"Travis Dickinson possesses that rare talent of combining high-level scholarship with a winsome ability to communicate to a popular audience. The result is material that one can trust will be accessible and based on solid research. *Wandering Toward God* is a beautiful example flowing from Dickinson's pen. For a long time, we have needed an informed, fresh new guide in navigating through stormy waters of doubt. Careful to distinguish doubt from unbelief and offering an extremely helpful definition of faith (ventured trust), Dickinson's book has it all. It begins with chapters that clarify doubt, faith, and related notions, along with locating the place of doubt in the process of spiritual growth. It moves on to discuss strategies for dealing with doubt, and it provides accessible answers to specific topics often involved in doubt. A truly wonderful book."

J. P. Moreland, Distinguished Professor of Philosophy at Talbot School of Theology, Biola University, and author of *A Simple Guide to Experience Miracles*

"In my work as a detective, doubt has always been a useful tool, especially when interviewing witnesses and potential suspects. If you believe everything you hear, you're unlikely to push past the initial claims and discover the truth. Doubt can play a similar role in motivating our spiritual investigations. Travis Dickinson's new book, *Wandering Toward God*, captures the important role doubt can play in our faith journey. This book will change the way you consider doubt, grow your confidence and comfort as you examine your own spiritual hesitation, and provide ample reason to trust the claims of Christianity. Every seeker and believer who has wrestled with doubt should read this book."

J. Warner Wallace, *Dateline*-featured cold-case detective and senior fellow at the Colson Center for Christian Worldview

"Beginning with a true story of being lost in a Wisconsin forest all the way to three final chapters on pithy aspects of the issues surrounding suffering and evil, this volume by Travis Dickinson packs a wallop. Since it's very well written in nontechnical language that moves quite quickly, the reader can jump on board with both feet. Short sentences spark the brain and keep things moving. Before long, it becomes obvious that a number of principles already have been communicated and are ready to be applied. I enjoyed it—highly recommended."

Gary R. Habermas, Distinguished Research Professor of Apologetics and Philosophy at Liberty University

"Travis Dickinson's *Wandering Toward God* is a superb guide to dealing with doubt. It is honest, insightful, nuanced, and practical. While many helpful books on the topic of doubt have been written, Dickinson provides us with a unique resource. He brings together a wide array of doubt-related themes and carefully arranges them into a well-crafted book—one that will serve doubters and other strugglers well as they wander and find their way back to God."

Paul Copan, Pledger Family Chair of Philosophy and Ethics at Palm Beach Atlantic University, and author of *Is God a Vindictive Bully?*

"What a masterful balance of clarity, accessibility, depth, and wisdom for anyone struggling with doubts about Christianity! *Wandering Toward God* is a perfect starting point for learning to think well about how to approach faith questions. It's filled with practical insights that will guide, equip, and encourage you on your journey of faith."

Natasha Crain, podcaster and author of *Faithfully Different*

"This is such a helpful guide to belief, doubt, and how to hold the Christian faith with confidence in a skeptical world. It is engaging, accessible, and honest. Anyone struggling with faith or seeking answers to their questions will find it a helpful road map to navigating a path toward God."

Justin Brierley, broadcaster and host of the *Unbelievable?* radio show and podcast

"With refreshing candor, *Wandering Toward God* offers an engaging corrective to pervasive mischaracterizations of faith and a helpful road map for navigating doubt with intellectual rigor. Using accessible illustrations drawn from both everyday life and Scripture, Dickinson affirms the tremendous value of faith seeking understanding and demonstrates a clear-minded, rational approach to common challenges leveled at Christianity. Those struggling with difficult questions will find encouragement and guidance— away from fear and confusion and toward a thoughtful, vibrant faith."

Melissa Cain Travis, author of *Science and the Mind of the Maker*

Travis Dickinson

Wandering Toward God

Finding Faith amid Doubts and Big Questions

An imprint of InterVarsity Press
Downers Grove, Illinois

InterVarsity Press
P.O. Box 1400 | Downers Grove, IL 60515-1426
ivpress.com | email@ivpress.com

InterVarsity Press® is the publishing division of InterVarsity Christian Fellowship/USA®. For more information, visit intervarsity.org.

All Scripture quotations, unless otherwise indicated, are taken from The Holy Bible, New International Version®, NIV®. Copyright © 1973, 1978, 1984, 2011 by Biblica, Inc.™ Used by permission of Zondervan. All rights reserved worldwide. www.zondervan.com. The "NIV" and "New International Version" are trademarks registered in the United States Patent and Trademark Office by Biblica, Inc.™

While any stories in this book are true, some names and identifying information may have been changed to protect the privacy of individuals.

The publisher cannot verify the accuracy or functionality of website URLs used in this book beyond the date of publication.

Cover design and image composite: David Fassett
Interior design: Daniel van Loon

ISBN 978-0-8308-4717-4 (print) | ISBN 978-0-8308-4718-1 (digital)

Printed in the United States of America ∞

Library of Congress Cataloging-in-Publication Data
Names: Dickinson, Travis, author.
Title: Wandering toward God: finding faith amid doubts and big questions /
  Travis Dickinson.
Description: Downers Grove, IL: InterVarsity Press, [2022] | Includes
  bibliographical references.
Identifiers: LCCN 2022024177 (print) | LCCN 2022024178 (ebook) | ISBN
  9780830847174 (print) | ISBN 9780830847181 (digital)
Subjects: LCSH: Faith.
Classification: LCC BT771.3 .D53 2022 (print) | LCC BT771.3 (ebook) | DDC
  234/.23—dc23/eng/20220706
LC record available at https://lccn.loc.gov/2022024177
LC ebook record available at https://lccn.loc.gov/2022024178

29 28 27 26 25 24 23 22 | 13 12 11 10 9 8 7 6 5 4 3 2 1

TO SHARI,

who is, to me, the fairest of them all.

AND TO KAELIA JOY, DELANEY GRACE, EMERY ANN, AND WILLIAM KADE.

May you journey well and find God.

Contents

Wandering but Not Lost

I wonder as I wander, out under the sky,
How Jesus the Savior did come for to die.

JOHN JACOB NILES

Not all who wander are lost.

J. R. R. TOLKIEN

I once was significantly lost. When I was a college student in northern Wisconsin, my dad and I were hiking on a trail that was somewhat familiar to me. I had been on this trail just a few weeks before and thought I would take us on a shortcut to get to some bluffs with a terrific view. It was, like many attempted shortcuts in life, a bad idea. We ended up getting off trail and wandering for a couple of terrifying hours. Then, all of a sudden, a man comes walking through the forest and we were saved! As it turns out he was deep in the forest scoping the land for a future hunting trip and we just happened to cross paths. We honestly wondered if he was an angel in disguise—it all felt a bit miraculous.

Wandering when lost is quite dangerous because you never know where you'll end up. Northern Wisconsin has thousands of miles of uninhabited forest. Had we gotten pointed in a different direction, I may not be here writing this sentence.

Now I'm not sure this man knew just where he was either. It took him a few moments to get his bearings. But there was an important difference between him and us. He had a compass and a map, and he knew the general direction of where we were.

Wandering can be scary. My dad and I were in a dangerous situation. But sometimes it's the best way to arrive at your destination. We can, like the man who saved us, wander with purpose. Life doesn't always give us a well-marked trail. We have to make our own way toward a destination. Wandering is not the problem, but wandering aimlessly is. There is risk of getting lost and we should take due caution, but the adventure is typically well worth the risk. Journeys like these profoundly change our lives.

In the novel *The Fellowship of the Ring* by J. R. R. Tolkien, there is a poem called the "Riddle of Strider." One stanza goes like this:

All that is gold does not glitter;
Not all who wander are lost.[1]

The poem is meant to convey a sense that things are not always as they appear. Things of value may come quite unexpectedly in dark figures like Strider and humble figures like hobbits.

One of Tolkien's most famous lines is "Not all who wander are lost." It's a great line, but what does it mean? It points to a winding journey filled with twists and turns but that's nonetheless intentional and traveled with purpose.

This is certainly true of the many journeys and adventures Tolkien beautifully describes in *The Lord of the Rings,* but it's also a lot like the journey of Christian faith. Now, we don't tend to associate wandering with faith, at least not in a positive light. But that's because many Christians have a rather thin notion of faith. For them, faith is just some decision we made along the way, not unlike the decision of where to go to college or what car to buy.

People identify with these decisions. Are you a Toyota person or is it Ford for you? Your being an alumnus of a certain university or college tends to follow you wherever you go. These things are identifying. You've joined the club.

Genuine faith, however, is not a *mere* decision, and you are not a mere member of a Christian club. To be sure, faith may begin with a decision. But it's a decision to begin a journey, an adventure, as we come to know the living God. It's a journey that is thrilling; sometimes terrifying and difficult (there are typically dragons along the way, as Tolkien would remind us) filled with twists, turns, suspense, drama; and times of both unimaginable joy and pain. Part of that journey of faith is the questions that come. Questions can sometimes turn into doubts. This, I suggest, is an important part of the journey of faith. We wander not as those who are lost but who are intentionally seeking God, encountering and pushing through challenges as they come. It's the only way to arrive at this destination.

Doubts and Big Questions

There I was in a seminary class, of all places, having a crisis of faith. We were only a few weeks into the semester, but I was seriously doubting my Christian beliefs. My growing-up experience was strongly Christian. If the church doors were open, my family was there, and we were involved. Generationally, my family had been doing formal ministry since at least my great-great-grandparents! And I was all-in from an early age. Somehow I made it through Sunday school, summer camp, youth group, countless youth events, Bible college, summer ministry, and international mission trips without deeply questioning my faith. I made a commitment to Christ at a young age and just assumed it was true from that point on. At this moment in seminary it hit me like a splash of ice-cold water—the kind that takes your breath away. I had never seriously considered *why* I should think Christianity is true above all other worldviews.

I'm sure as a kid I asked questions along the way. But there's a difference between considering the truth of Christianity when everyone knows the answer (or think they do) and deeply considering its truth with a real possibility of its being wrong. There's the *Let's have a fun discussion about Christianity* sort of considering. And then there's the painful, teary-eyed, scared to death struggle of considering whether it's really true. I had never done the latter until I found myself doubting in seminary.

It is quite common for Christians to experience doubts from time to time. Unfortunately, doubts about our Christian beliefs are often treated in the same way we would treat a common cold. We wait it out, treat symptoms as best as we can (perhaps with a good dose of prayer and Bible study), and hope it goes away. This approach might work for some. But for many others, the doubts creep back in and they return with friends! As the doubts compound, Christianity can begin to feel uncompelling for this reason alone. Notice, it's not for a lack of evidence. It's simply because there are doubts that are left untreated. Sadly, many abandon their Christian faith because they cannot find a safe place to admit and talk about their doubts. Rather than our questions and doubts being a part of the adventure as we wander toward God, without a safe place to doubt our faith Christianity can feel like a fake.

My story is different. I leaned into my doubts. I asked those difficult questions in a lonely backroom of a church I had been given to work in while in seminary. I began to read. I had conversations with people further along in their journey than I was. I began to find answers. Even though I still had plenty of questions (and still do today), I began to see my way clear of some problems. I didn't fall away. In fact, my faith grew stronger. The irony is, I became even more well-grounded in my faith. By leaning into my doubts, I came to a place of deeper faith.

Doubting While Faithful

How about you? Do you have questions? Are you seeking and searching? Are you doubting? If you have questions about Christianity or are struggling with doubt, I want you to know that *you are normal!* Hear this: *You. Are. Normal.* The honest struggle of questions and doubts is not sin. You are not failing. You are courageous—probably more courageous than others who act like they have it all figured out. I respect you. It's most likely that you are doubting your faith precisely because you are intellectually honest and are seeking truth rather than mere acceptance by your peers. This can be a lonely place, but please hear me: *You are not alone!* Some of the most ardent defenders of the Christian faith wandered toward God with doubts and big questions.

For others who, like me growing up, have never really considered the reasons why you should believe; it's time to do so.

Let me be clear. I don't want you to doubt your faith just for the sake of doubting it. Though doubting and deconstructing faith is a popular thing these days and leaning into doubt can lead to good things (such as a well-grounded faith), doubt is not good as an end in itself. But I do want you to ask questions. And hard questions often lead to having some doubts along the way. It isn't always easy. But here's the good news: you are reading a book that sees having doubts and big questions as perfectly compatible with having faith and is a normal and valuable part of the journey to a deeply grounded faith.

We don't want to stay in the grip of doubt. Again, doubt is not the destination. We may be wandering but we are wandering *toward* God. God is the destination. To be a bit more accurate, truth is the destination. Doubting forces us to take a careful look at what's true. I found God waiting for me. I was wandering, to be sure, but I was wandering in pursuit of God.

Doubting from Six Miles Up

Let's talk about airplanes. While flying on an airplane is quite commonplace today, it's almost absurd when you stop to think about it. We strap into a little seat in this huge metal craft, drive down a little road, and lift off into the atmosphere! We can cross oceans and continents in a matter of hours. People of a previous era would be awestruck or would perhaps not even believe this is a real thing.

As extraordinary as it is, most of us don't know much about the science of flight. We haven't a clue about how a large and heavy aircraft can lift off the tarmac into the sky. But many of us get on board and are so confident and relaxed that we may even take a nap. We entrust our whole lives to the process (that is, we entrust ourselves to the airplane and the pilots, mechanics, engineers, and so on). Unless you are the sort of person who packs a parachute in your carry-on, you can't sort of or partly entrust yourself to an airplane when you fly. It's your whole life or you don't get on. And though airplanes are relatively safe, there is a big risk to this. When things go wrong on an airplane, they typically go *very* wrong!

Let's suppose you and I are sitting in the airport awaiting an upcoming flight, and someone approaches and begins to raise all kinds of questions designed to cast doubt on us getting on board.

THEM Are you about to get on this airplane?

US (looking around to make sure he's talking to us) Uh, yes, we are.

THEM Do you know how airplanes work?

US (sheepishly smiling) Well, not really.

THEM Really? And you are about to get on board?

US Yeah.

THEM Do you know at what altitude the airplane cruises?

US I think we heard the captain say something about 30,000 feet.

THEM Yes! You realize that's about six miles off the planet, right?

US Never thought of it that way.

THEM It's a 747, right?

US I guess so.

THEM Do you know how much a 747 weighs?

US Uh, no, but I'm guessing a lot.

THEM	Yes, a lot! A 747 weighs in at about one million pounds!
US	Really? That *is* a lot.
THEM	Do you know what an airplane is made of?
US	Well it looks like it's mostly made of metal.
THEM	Right. It's a million pounds of mostly metal.
US	(looking at each other with a little anxiety) Wow.
THEM	Do you know how many processes have to be timed precisely for the airplane to fly through the air?
US	(simply shaking our heads)
THEM	Thousands!
US	(We both gulp)
THEM	Here's the big question: Does it make any sense that a craft made of mostly metal, weighing a million pounds, with thousands of processes that must be timed perfectly can lift off the ground and fly through the air at six miles off the planet? Are you willing to entrust yourself to this?

We both begin to feel nervous. We're intellectually struggling a bit with how an airplane doesn't just fall out of the sky.

But here's the thing. When my seat section is called, I'm going to get on the airplane despite these doubts. And I bet you would too (especially if we are going somewhere tropical with a beach)! This is because, even if we can't answer the person's questions and even if this fact creates an intellectual struggle within us, we typically (and this is key) know enough about airplanes to rationally get on board. That is, we may not know how it all works, but most of us have sufficiently good reason from experience, both ours and others', to get on board despite our doubts. We could even be on board the airplane, cruising at 30,000 feet in the air, entrusting our very lives to it, and continue to struggle with these questions. We are having doubts about flying—while flying!

When it comes to faith, most of us jump on board not because we have it all figured out but because we know enough to trust Christ. We had the gospel presented to us, the Spirit of God moved in our lives and we placed trust—but we still have lots of questions. The mere presence of an unanswered question or even a few doubts should not destroy faith any more than our unanswered questions about flying should keep us from our tropical beach.

With these things in mind, if you are doubting your faith, I want to encourage you to take a deep breath. Your faith need not hang in the balance only if you can somehow get rid of all your doubts by the end of the day. This pressurizes the situation and keeps you from being able to think clearly about the questions you have. So let me take some pressure off. You can question and even doubt your faith while entrusting your life to the truth of Christianity.

Doubt Versus Unbelief

Why is this? Faith and doubt are consistent because, as Os Guinness points out, "Doubt is not the opposite of faith. Unbelief is."[2] Having doubts, even serious doubts, does not mean you don't have faith. Faith and doubt are not opposites like black and white. In fact, doubt seems to require some measure of faith or at least belief. Think about it: if you didn't believe in Christianity, then there would be nothing to doubt. We doubt those things we still believe until we resolve the doubt or we stop believing. So doubt only makes sense in the context of belief and faith.

Now we may go from a place of doubt to a place of unbelief. In the Bible the term *unbelief* is often used in a particular way. It's not the mere lack of a belief. As Guinness puts it, unbelief "is usually used of a willful refusal to believe or of a deliberate decision to disobey." He goes on, "Unbelief is a state of mind that is closed against God, an attitude of heart that disobeys God as much as it disbelieves the truth. Unbelief is the consequence of a settled choice."[3] Guinness makes the point that unbelief is an act of the will.

When it comes to doubt, in its most basic sense, we don't typically choose to doubt. We make choices in light of our doubts, but whether we struggle with doubt in a particular area is not typically up to us.

It's much like the distinction between feelings of affection and acts of love. We can't just choose to feel affection for someone, but we do choose to act lovingly. The feelings of affection may come and go, but we may choose to love someone even if we are not "feelin' it" at a particular moment. We can of course make choices that help cultivate or change our feelings of affection with, say, a family member who's hard to love. But the feelings themselves are not directly up to us.

Doubt is like this. We may start to struggle a bit as we ask deep and difficult questions about our faith. In this, we are not choosing to struggle. This is just how it strikes us. We can choose to investigate our doubts or just ignore them, hoping they go away. That is, we have many choices in light of the doubts, and our choices may lead us to a place of greater or lesser doubts. However, doubts arise in us when we have questions we can't answer and we begin to struggle with this. We can choose unbelief and intellectually ignore or walk away, or we can choose faith. Faith is the opposite of unbelief in that we choose (as we'll see in chap. 4) to lean in and venture in trust rather than willfully refusing to believe.

I can illustrate the distinction between doubt and unbelief with the story of the apostle Thomas. Though he is often labeled as "doubting" Thomas, his issue is not mere doubt (see John 20:24-29). It seems to be a struggle with unbelief. As the story goes, Thomas was the only one who wasn't present to see the risen Jesus when he first appeared to the disciples (John 20:19-23). Imagine how you would feel if you were Thomas. The person he had committed his life to in discipleship has just been shamefully executed. He thought this was going to be a movement in which Jesus, as the Jewish Messiah, would become king of Israel. But it didn't happen. Jesus is dead. Or at least he was dead. As it turns out, every one of Jesus' closest followers sees Jesus risen from the dead—except Thomas. When the other disciples tell Thomas they have seen the Lord, Thomas doesn't only want to see the risen Jesus but also wants to put his finger into his wounds! He demands it, otherwise, as he says, "I will not believe" (v. 25).

We don't know all of what was going on in the heart of Thomas; however, it looks like he has become stubborn and raised the intellectual stakes considerably. Perhaps he is feeling hurt in being left out. In any case, he doesn't seem to be struggling with doubts about what he believes as much as refusing to believe. It's not as if he's weighing the evidence and is not yet convinced. He disregards the testimonial evidence of his closest friends. In the face of their testimony he says he will never believe unless he gets what the other disciples got—and more. This, it seems to me, is not a mere intellectual battle of the mind. It's the stubbornness of the heart.

The core struggle of doubt, on the other hand, is not willful; it is not a choice. If we had a choice, most of us would never choose to doubt. By its nature it's a struggle with what to believe, which is often an unenjoyable place to be. If we could shake the doubts, we would.

Eyeing the Ledge of Faith

Not long ago I was a speaker at a camp, and the activity for the day was rappelling down a rock face. Rappelling is rock climbing in reverse. We start from the top of a rock face, are strapped in by ropes, and walk backward (or, if we are experienced, jump backward) down the rock face, letting out rope as we go. Someone below us is also holding the rope in case we start to fall. So there's very little possibility of actually falling, but here's the thing: when we first learn to rappel, we feel like we are going to fall at almost every moment, especially getting over the first ridge of the rock face. It can be quite terrifying.

Every time I have gone rappelling with students, there are always three kinds of people. The first—call this person Suzy—gets strapped in and without hesitation scoots down the rock. She is supremely confident. It may be because she is a thrill seeker and just doesn't have inhibitions about such things. But, for the sake of the analogy, let's assume Suzy has rappelled before. This is old hat for her, and her confidence is because she knows from experience the ropes will hold her securely and can be trusted.

The second, we'll call him Larry, is nervous, but he does go down. Larry has never done this before and hesitates, has deep doubts about whether it's a good idea to be on a rock face at that moment, and has to be coaxed down the rock face, perhaps every step of the way. Notice Larry is not choosing to be fearful here. It seems clear that if Larry could be confident, he would choose to be confident. He's having an internal battle and, at moments, his decision to go down hangs in the balance. But Larry chooses to go down despite the internal battle. While he doesn't scoot down the rock face quickly, as Suzy did, both Suzy and Larry had faith. Suzy was a lot more confident in placing her faith in the ropes, the harness, the clips, and the person on the ground holding the ropes. Larry struggled, but he also chose to have faith in these things. Suzy's experience is the more mature experience. If Larry continues rappelling, then he will likely get there at some point. But the point is they both go down the mountain face!

Contrast these to a third person, John. John gets to the top and looks over the edge and says, "Uh, no way," and refuses to go down. There is almost always one or two in the group who get to the top of the rock face but refuse to go a step further, and no amount of coaxing can get them to even consider strapping into the ropes, much less trust that they'll hold them up. John may have an internal battle in a way similar to Larry, but John chooses to stay on the ground that is horizontal rather than go vertical over the rock edge. While Suzy and Larry make the same decision, John's decision is different. John chooses not to rappel at all. John chooses not to place his faith in the ropes, harness, and so on.

People who are struggling with doubt are in a struggle similar to Larry's. It's not an enjoyable place to be in the midst of the battle, but there can be important life lessons to be had in those moments. Larry and John are probably somewhat envious of Suzy's confidence. But they are new to this and are also human beings. It's part of the human experience to struggle from time to time. Just like Larry and John don't choose to struggle with fear, we don't simply choose to struggle with our doubts. But, like Larry, we can choose to move toward faith as we face our doubts, even if it is inch by inch.

This book is designed for people like Larry who are eyeing the ledge of faith. It is not aiming to convince the committed non-Christian. If a person, like John, refuses to move even one inch toward the ledge, then what we say here will not be very helpful. Unfortunately, this is the all-too-common experience with many committed atheists. Just as many religious believers are unwilling to question their religious beliefs, many atheists seem unwilling to genuinely consider their possibility. These are often paradigm cases of unbelief. While I hope the committed atheist (as well as religious believers) will consider having an open mind, the focus here is for someone willing to honestly look at the case for faith.

We face a rock ledge with a steep drop. Fear and trepidation are quite normal and caution is appropriate. I will not be recommending a wild and incautious leap of faith over the edge. It's typically a bad idea to leap over a rock ledge with no knowledge or reasons to believe it will go well. And I don't think God expects this either when it comes to faith. While we do ultimately stake it all on the reality of God, faith shouldn't be an irrational leap. Don't get me wrong, there will be plenty of instances when we will have to trust in the face of uncertainty and when we are intimidated and being pulled in the opposite direction. Faith takes courage, and there's always a risk. Despite our fears, we'll need to choose to inch our way toward the ledge and peer over. We'll need to lean into the ropes. And in my experience with rappelling as well as Christian faith, those ropes hold strong. It can be terrifying, but taste and see that the Lord is good and he's there and he's worthy of our complete trust.

This is a book for searchers and seekers who are quite open to coming down the rock face even though they are facing the obstacles of unanswered questions and doubts. I am assuming that if you are doubting Christianity, you believe but you're in the midst of intellectual tension. You are at the crossroads, and perhaps the only clear thing is that the path forward is unclear. If that's you, welcome to the journey. It's going to involve some wandering, but it's well worth the trip as we wander toward God.

Doubt Defined

Now that I am a Christian, I do have moods in which the whole thing looks very improbable: but when I was an atheist I had moods in which Christianity looked terribly probable.

C. S. Lewis

There are many faces of doubt. Sometimes it is only a momentary stumble along the way. We can doubt a belief we don't even care much about, and it's no big deal. Other times, it is an all-consuming cage fight to the death, involving our most cherished beliefs.

The word *doubt* itself is used in a variety of ways both in the Bible and in casual conversations. It is sometimes used to refer to something that is entirely intellectual. Other times it is used to describe certain emotional states or even a moral attitude.

I will not be attempting to describe all the many forms in which doubt may show up.[1] Rather, I aim to think about the basic core of an experience of doubt. Before it becomes emotionally spring-loaded and before it results in moral attitudes, doubt, at its core, is an honest intellectual tension. It begins here but can then manifest and morph in many different ways. Doubt can manifest in sinful behavior, but it need not. Doubt can manifest as being tossed about like a wave of the sea

(James 1:6). But it doesn't necessarily have to. Doubt can even manifest as radical skepticism or lead to unbelief, but it certainly does not need to. If we dial all that back, I suggest we are left with an intellectual tension where one of our beliefs seems like it might be false. This is the core experience of doubt.

Consider the rappelling example of chapter one. The conception of doubt that I'm focused on is analogous to the internal struggle a person has while anxiously eyeing the rock ledge. It is analogous because, though our struggle on the rock ledge can play out in several ways, it all seems to spring from that internal battle. Similarly, on the journey of faith the core of doubt is that internal battle we have as we work out what to believe and where to place our trust.

The root of our English term *doubt* has to do with duplicity. It is being divided or doubled up in our thinking. But this isn't a matter of simply being confused or unable to make up our mind or having inconsistent beliefs. Doubt is the experience of tension between what we believe and some contrary claim we don't yet believe. Doubt is the experience of feeling the force or draw of that contrary claim. From here it may manifest in many different ways. But this is the core. Put simply, doubt is when one of our beliefs seems like it might be false.

Three Dimensions of Doubt

This gives us three basic dimensions of doubt. The first is that doubt always involves something we believe. As was said in chapter one, we doubt something we already believe. If there was no belief in view, then it wouldn't be doubt. We can doubt all sorts of beliefs. It may be beliefs about God's existence, the truth of Christianity, the reliability of an automobile, the date of my next doctor's appointment, the moral character of a political candidate, the state of the economy, or whether I turned my oven off before leaving the house. But if we are doubting, there is some belief in view that we are doubting.

The second dimension is there is always a contrary claim in view that's causing the tension. Let's say we believe that the Christian God exists. The contrary claim could be that there's no God at all. Or it could be that a different version of God exists, say, the God of Islam. Both of these are contrary to the claim that the Christian God exists in that if either of these were true, the belief that the Christian God exists would be false. It's important to note that the contrary claim here is not yet believed. We believe that the Christian God exists when we doubt the existence of the Christian God, but we have in view a contrary claim that's giving us some trouble.

Doubt is really the felt tension that exists between a belief you have and a contrary claim you do not yet believe. The contrary claim is starting to seem somewhat plausible, and this creates a tension. The third dimension is what is sometimes, in philosophy, called a seeming state. This isn't a mere feeling or emotion but rather a kind of intuition or an experience of assertive force. It's that experience of, on hearing a compelling case for a claim, the claim *seems* plausibly true. A good salesperson knows how to make a claim *seem* true even when it clearly isn't. Or consider a compelling theory that makes you question what you've always believed. Even if it is a somewhat wild theory, it makes it seem like your belief is false.

Simply put, doubt is that experience of one of our beliefs seeming like it might be false: it's less plausible. Some contrary claim begins to seem like it's got something going for it. You don't believe any of it yet, but it's starting to seem like it might be so. This is the internal battle of doubt.

Imagine you are watching a baseball game with a friend. The two of you are great friends, but you are rooting for opposite teams. Let's say your team is doing quite well. As it gets into the late innings, your team is up by five runs. At this moment it seems to all that this team is going to win. Nothing is guaranteed, of course, especially in baseball. It's still possible for the other team to rally and win the game, but it *seems* like they won't.

Imagine your friend came to the game confidently believing that his team was going to be victorious. As the innings stretch on and his team starts to go down by a point or two, he still believes, but it begins to *seem* as if his belief may be false. At this moment he begins to doubt. As we get to the late innings with a few more runs scored by the other team, it's still possible for his team to win and he still believes they can, but it likely doesn't seem very plausible anymore. Your friend is in the throes of doubt. The belief he has strongly seems as if it is false.

Seemings come in degrees. It can seem just a bit implausible, or it can seem completely false. We still have the belief while we doubt, whatever it is, but it begins to seem problematic or unjustified. Often doubts come because we feel the pull or force of an objection to one of our beliefs. This is the seesaw of competing claims. We often begin to doubt when an objection to one of our beliefs begins to seem plausible. The more plausible the objection seems, the less plausible our belief will seem and vice versa. Most of us have had the experience of being rather confident in one of our beliefs until we come to a plausible objection. All of a sudden we start to doubt our belief when we feel the pull of that objection. We experience this duplicity in that intellectual tension. We experience doubt.

Remember the old science-fiction movies when the spaceships always came equipped with a tractor beam? If we fly too close to a larger ship, we may get caught in the tractor beam. It pulls us in with an invisible force. When we doubt, we, in a way, find ourselves in the tractor beam of an objection. There's a contrary claim that sounds all too plausible, and it makes trouble for one of our beliefs. Again, it can be a slight pull or an overwhelming force.

This is when our intellectual struggles start. We are often quite comfortable in our beliefs until some contrary claim starts to seem plausible and draw us in. It's that nagging sense that may start in the background and makes us question whether our belief is wrong. It's that proverbial pebble in our shoe bothering us at every step. Again, this intellectual tension can grow and manifest in many different ways. But at its core, it is when one of our beliefs seems as if it might be false.

Understanding doubt this way sheds light on why we can have doubts and still have faith. It's not that uncommon for us to experience a bit of uncertainty about one of our beliefs. This is going to happen as we ask big questions and honestly consider objections to our beliefs. As we look at an objection, if it is a good objection, we'll likely feel a bit of the force of that objection. We might think, *Wow, never thought of that before,* as we experience some intellectual tension. But it is not as if we immediately stop believing. Again, this assumes we still believe—because believing is an ingredient of doubt. We can experience the tractor beam of an objection while believing that Christianity is true and placing our faith in Christ. In fact, to abandon the faith just because there are some unanswered questions would be intellectually irresponsible. The responsible thing to do is to maintain our belief as we further investigate the objection.

The Big or Small Struggle of Doubt

So here's the picture: you believe something to be true. Let's say you believe that God exists. But then you encounter an objection to that belief. Perhaps someone presents you with a reason to believe that God does not exist. Let's say the argument is compelling and you don't know how to answer the challenge. That moment is uncomfortable. You are feeling the force of this contrary claim, and it seems as if your belief might be false. You still believe God exists. But there's now intellectual tension here. You are divided in your thinking.

Doubt in this case is likely a big deal and we may be in for a deep struggle. But doubts do not need to be all that big of a struggle. Perhaps as I reflect on the objection, it quickly becomes clear that, despite how it first appeared, it is not a compelling objection. The objection turns out to be easily resolved. Or sometimes we don't care all that much about the belief. Let's say I confidently believe I have a doctor's appointment at 2:30 p.m. on March 12. But my wife assures me the appointment is at 2:30 p.m. on March 22 instead. My wife is almost always right on these kinds of things, so I now doubt that my appointment is on March 12. But the belief isn't very important to me. It doesn't bother me (too much) to (eventually) concede (as often happens) and believe that my wife is right (because she's almost always right).

By contrast, when we are doubting a cherished belief and it's not easily resolved, this can be extremely disconcerting. We begin to feel like this belief we have relied on and at times organized our life around may be wrong. This can be difficult indeed.

This is true of our Christian beliefs, but it can also hold true for an atheist. C. S. Lewis recounts his conversion experience as one of total resistance. In a chapter titled "Checkmate" in his autobiography, Lewis says,

> I gave in, and admitted that God was God, and knelt and prayed: perhaps, that night, the most dejected and reluctant convert in all England. I did not then see what is now the most shining and obvious thing; the Divine humility which will accept a convert even on such terms. The Prodigal Son at least walked home on his own feet. But who can duly adore that Love which will open the high gates to a prodigal who is brought in kicking, struggling, resentful, and darting his eyes in every direction for a chance of escape?[2]

For Lewis, it began with doubts about his atheism and eventually led him to Christ.

We can feel very upset about the doubts we have, or we can feel indifferent or even happy and relieved about them. Suppose you tragically have a diagnosis for a fatal disease and are given six weeks to live. You believe that this is it for you. But imagine the relief and joy to begin to find counterevidence to this diagnosis. Even when it is a slim chance, you will likely welcome such doubts.

Why We Doubt

It's all too common for Christians to think of doubt as nothing more than a sinful choice where we refuse to trust God. Admittedly, doubts may be a part of this picture. But as we've defined things, this is unbelief. A struggle with doubts very well could have played a role in someone coming to a place of unbelief, but this would have involved choices beyond the experience of doubt. I've argued that doubt is not itself a sinful choice. It's also not the case that to doubt is to fail to trust God. As we've already said, doubt may manifest as a lack of trust, but it doesn't have to. We can have doubts while fully trusting God.

But let's be clear. Even if doubt is not a willful choice, it is the *result* of a fallen and sinful world. The Bible makes clear that the world is not how it should be. We have desires, drives, temptations, insecurities, and attractions that are not necessarily a matter of our choices but are the result of our fallenness and often lead to sinful choices. These are the consequences of living in a fallen world. We are even depraved or corrupted in our thinking (Romans 1:28). There's something deep inside of us that doesn't want God to exist or Jesus to be Lord, and this may lead us to have an internal intellectual battle. The point is that doubt may not be an explicitly sinful choice; but it does spring from our fallen and sinful state.

However, as Alister McGrath reminds us,

It is not entirely correct to describe doubt as simply due to human *sinfulness*. It is also a reflection of human frailty. We are human beings, and quite frankly, this means that we operate under limits. . . . We're like grasshoppers, trying to make sense of a vast universe (Isaiah 40:22).[3]

Doubt, at its core, is also a very natural result of our attempting to make our way in a vast world. Doubts arise from asking big questions. And we need to ask big questions about the world and reality to make our way in it. We may be grasshoppers trying to understand a vast universe, but we are curious grasshoppers, often with the need to figure things out as best we can. We are going to ask big questions. And sometimes these big questions are going to cause us to struggle.

Doubt and the Bible

It's also not uncommon for Christians to think that the Bible takes a dim view of doubt. Does the Bible see doubt as necessarily bad? Let's look at a few passages.

At one point in Jesus' ministry Peter steps out of a perfectly good boat onto the water. Jesus comes to the disciples while walking on the water, and Peter requests to join Jesus there. Matthew 14: 29-31 says, "Peter got down out of the boat, walked on the water and came toward Jesus. But when he saw the wind, he was afraid and, beginning to sink, cried out, 'Lord, save me!' Immediately Jesus reached out his hand and caught him. 'You of little faith,' he said, 'why did you doubt?'"

Peter is miraculously walking on water. Let's not let that slip by us. The disciples at first think that Jesus is a ghost and they are terrified (Matthew 14:26). But Peter gets the idea that if it is Jesus, then Jesus could miraculously cause Peter to walk on the water. But as he's walking on the water, Peter starts looking around and finds some extremely compelling reasons that suggest walking on the water in a storm is not such a good idea. In that brief moment he struggles and quickly cedes his trust away from Christ. Jesus chides Peter for lacking faith and asks why he doubted.

Should we conclude from this that doubt is a bad thing? Peter fails in this situation, and we certainly shouldn't model ourselves on Peter's example here. There's a clear sense in which Peter shouldn't have doubted. But considering the extreme circumstances he's in, having some doubts seems natural enough. The mistake, I'd suggest, is that Peter chose not to trust Christ. He had plenty of good reasons to trust Christ despite the doubts he may have been experiencing.

It was a fail on Peter's part, but it was also a powerful lesson. Peter and Jesus get back in the boat, and Jesus proceeds to calm a storm (don't skip that either!). If he wasn't convinced before, Peter learns that Jesus does indeed have the power to cause him to walk on water and that he has power over the weather. Peter also learns an important lesson about faith. In one short narrative Peter sees who Jesus is, how Peter is supposed to rely on him, and what happens when he doesn't.

This passage teaches us that we should trust Christ despite the circumstances we face. Jesus has control over the waters and even over the storm. But Peter reasonably experienced some doubts in these circumstances and failed to place his trust in Christ. He had "little faith." This passage doesn't teach us that we shouldn't have internal battles. These are going to come even if we don't want them to. But we should come out the other side of this battle trusting Christ.

Another passage that seems to take a dim view of doubt is in the book of James. James tells us that if we lack wisdom, we should ask God. He then says, "When you ask, you must believe and not doubt, because the one who doubts is like a wave of the sea, blown and tossed by the wind. That person should not expect to receive anything from the Lord. Such a person is double-minded and unstable in all they do" (James 1:6-8).

It's important to understand that James is addressing a particular manifestation of doubt rather than the basic notion of doubt that I've focused on. James is not talking about a mere internal battle. The word he uses here for doubt is best understood as allowing doubt to produce unstable and divided behavior. As one New Testament commentator puts it, "The word suggests . . . not so much intellectual doubt as a basic conflict in loyalties."[4] Having an internal battle of doubt may lead to a conflict in whom you choose to be loyal to, but it doesn't have to. That is, doubt may manifest in a disloyal attitude toward God and, when it does, we shouldn't expect to receive anything from the Lord.

But even with this in mind, the broader point to be made is that doubting is not where we want to end up. We want to ask in faith with no doubting. And while we may not find ourselves walking on water (at least not very often!), we nevertheless don't want to sink in the sea when we are in the midst of a storm. We want to have a mature Christian faith. But this is the ideal we aim at. We are not always going to achieve the ideal. And there are important and valuable lessons when we stumble and go through times of doubt.

Other passages in the Bible have an understanding view toward those who are struggling with doubt. Take, for example, Matthew 28:17. Jesus has risen from the dead and has gathered his disciples to commission and send them out. This is the culmination of the narrative in the Gospel of Matthew. Jesus has conquered death and is sending out his disciples to make disciples of all nations. As they gather on the mountain and just before he gives this commission, it says, "When they saw him, they worshiped him; but some doubted."

Why mention this just before Jesus' final words? This, it seems, is simply an honest report about where some of his disciples were at. Those who doubted are not condemned or rebuked. Instead, Jesus proceeds to commission them, including those who doubted, to make disciples throughout the whole world.

Perhaps the clearest passage that expresses and even calls for concern in regard to those who struggle intellectually is in the book of Jude. In this short epistle, Jude clearly distinguishes between certain ungodly members of their community who "deny Jesus Christ our only Sovereign and Lord" (v. 4) and others who need compassion. He outright condemns the former. But, in stark contrast, he encourages his readers to "be merciful to those who doubt" (v. 22). He even closes the epistle with encouraging statements that seem to have doubters in mind. He gives glory to God "who is able to keep you from stumbling and to present you before his glorious presence without fault and with great joy" (v. 24).

Finally, it's important to see that the Bible includes many who struggle with intellectual tensions without condemnation. For example, throughout the book of Psalms and other poetic literature, a familiar refrain is crying out frustration and confusion. Job suffers in the tension that he hadn't sinned against God and yet was suffering as if he had. David in the Psalms and many of the Old Testament prophets repeatedly cry out, not understanding why the wicked flourish and God's people suffer. Even John the Baptist wonders whether Jesus is truly the Messiah or if they should expect another. We have often seen many Christians throughout history—from Saint Augustine to Martin Luther to Francis Schaeffer to Mother Teresa to Billy Graham—struggling through big questions and doubts. The honest wandering of the heart and mind is simply part of the picture of how humans relate to God. This is in part due to our fallenness, finitude, and frailty. But what do we do with the reality that we are fallen, finite, and frail? Run away? Ignore it? Take a blind and irrational leap? I suggest doubts are a normal part of the Christian experience, and there is value in leaning into our doubts as we wander toward God.

The Value of Doubt

When we ask whether doubting is a good thing, the answer then is a bit complicated. In one sense, the answer is no, doubting is not a good thing. It is a struggle that results from a fallen world and the frailty of our minds. This is why the celebration of doubt and deconstruction popular among some Christians is wrongheaded. If we think Christianity is true, there's no reason necessarily to be happy about and celebrate a serious case of doubt. But, in another sense, there's value in doubt when it is handled properly.

The first thing to see is that an experience of doubt is often quite humbling. Our doubts often pull us back to earth when we are in a place of overconfidence. Alvin Plantinga once humorously remarked, "Most of us form estimates of our intelligence, wisdom, and moral fiber that are considerably higher than an objective estimate would warrant; no doubt 90 percent of us think ourselves well above average along these lines."[5]

The point is that though we are often rather confident in our ability to believe truly, we can be and often are wrong about things. Our doubts help us stay grounded and have a more accurate estimation.

Second, our doubts can help us pinpoint the pressure points—the weaker parts—of our views. Asking the big questions is important for our faith. Through asking questions we can achieve the great good of growing in our confidence and our knowledge of the world. But this is almost always going to involve some struggle with doubts along the way. As such, doubts work as signposts to where more investigation is needed. Frederick Buechner says that "doubts are the ants in the pants of faith."[6] Tim Keller observes that doubts function for faith in a way similar to antibodies in the human body.[7] These both make a similar point. Doubts have value as a kind of corrective for our faith in areas we need to think more carefully about. Nobody likes to have ants in their pants! But having ants in our pants does motivate us. When we are comfortable in our faith, we tend to take things for granted.

This is especially true for those of us who live in a Christian bubble. There were points in my growing up experience when I'm not sure I knew a non-Christian. Consequently, my faith was rarely challenged and was surprisingly fragile. Here's the irony: once I struggled with serious doubts, my faith became sure and well-grounded. But this is because I leaned into my doubts and asked the big questions. The doubts motivated me to search for answers. When we ignore our doubts or simply try to stop doubting, we miss an opportunity for growth. Faith that has not been refined by questions and doubts is likely not strong. By investigating our doubts, we press in more deeply to our faith. This, it seems to me, is a great value indeed.

Now, this is a bit scary and intimidating. But if the Christian faith is true and reasonable (as I'm convinced it is), then we will find answers to these questions. This isn't to say that we will resolve all issues; we all have to live with some unanswered questions. In my journey I had to find answers to a few questions that were deep and difficult. But I did find those answers. And I went on to ask other questions, but I did so with fewer doubts and more confidence. I still have questions, which I wrestle with as I continue the journey, but my faith is well-grounded in a broad base of evidence that I think makes Christianity extremely compelling. I couldn't, at this point, walk away from the Christian faith with intellectual honesty. I'm far from perfect, but the contrary claims don't have the pull that they once did. But this is because I've weighed the evidence and I have a confident faith.

The Risk of Doubt

You might be thinking this all sounds a bit risky. And you're right. Investigating and attempting to address our doubt does indeed open us to the possibility of concluding that our beliefs are false. I'm not going to sugarcoat that. There is risk here. It's entirely possible that as someone digs into the investigation of their doubts, they come out the other side unbelieving. Full stop. We'd be fools to think this does not happen. But the case for Christianity is a good one, and too many Christians are unaware of the case. In some ways the problem is not that we have too many doubting their faith, but that we don't have enough people serious enough about their faith to ask the big questions! Consequently there's a serious lack of Christians able to provide thoughtful answers to those questions. Those who are doubting are at least on the journey and asking the questions. And I'll make a case for how to doubt well and how to ask the big questions (see chaps. 5–6). If it's done well, I think we find compelling answers.

But more importantly, even though it's risky, ignoring doubt is no less risky. Many folks walk away from the faith not so much because the evidence against Christianity was so overwhelming, but because they don't find people authentically open to think about and address their deep questions. They find people who say, "You just gotta have faith!" and when the questions get a bit annoying they might be told to knock it off. But when it comes to doubting our faith, most of us can't simply knock it off. This dismissive attitude often leads to emotional hurt and confusion, and consequently people walk away. I'm no psychologist, but when I hear so-called deconversion stories, being rebuffed for asking hard questions seems all too often to feature in the person's decision to walk away.

Here's my contention: Christianity is true, and it can handle your questions. I of course don't want anyone to walk away from the faith. But there's no way to ensure this doesn't happen. Though I have had significant doubts, I've investigated and have found Christianity to be extremely compelling and Jesus peerless. I can't guarantee this will be your experience as well, but I invite you to take a deep look. Christians stand in a rich tradition of taking the hardest objections to Christianity and offering thoughtful and honest responses.[8] I find it completely tragic that folks walk when they haven't even considered the great heritage of answers to their questions. If you've doubted your faith, you are not alone. You stand among a great cloud of those asking similar questions and attesting to the truth and reality of Christianity.

Certainty Is a House of Cards

**The demand for certainty is one which is natural to man,
but is nevertheless an intellectual vice.**

BERTRAND RUSSELL

**Doubt is not a pleasant condition,
but certainty is an absurd one.**

VOLTAIRE

**Surely, while we teach that faith ought to be certain and assured,
we cannot imagine any certainty that is not tinged with doubt,
or any assurance that is not assailed by some anxiety.**

JOHN CALVIN

A re you certain about that?"
This can sometimes be a difficult question. When it comes to our faith, we often don't want to concede uncertainty. It is sometimes thought that Christians are called to a complete certainty in our Christian faith. Nothing less will do. But we often fall short of certainty. We naturally long for it, but all it takes are some questions and doubts, and suddenly our sense of certainty has slipped through our fingers.

In this chapter I suggest that certainty is *not* what we should aim for in our journey toward Christian faith. Doing so sets us up to fail when questions inevitably come and our faith falls like a house of cards.

What Is Certainty?

The word *certainty* is often used to say that a matter is settled for a person. Someone might ask, "Are you certain Jones is the best candidate for the upcoming political election?" If you say, "Yes, I'm absolutely certain. Jones is my guy!" you likely would be saying your mind is made up about voting for Jones and the issue is, for you, settled.

We do often have our minds made up about such things, but can we ever be *completely* settled in these matters? Can we have ruled out *all* relevant possibilities where Jones is not the best candidate? Isn't it possible that we've overlooked something?

Okay, time out! You may have just rolled your eyes a bit. Asking such pedantic questions is precisely how philosophers get a bad rap. Admittedly it can sometimes be annoying to be pressed to consider unlikely possibilities, and philosophers do love to ask these sorts of questions. But it's *really* important here that we understand the status of our Christian claims. As we'll see, if there is some possibility of error (i.e., certainty is not possible), a consideration of evidence becomes extremely important. So hang on as we ask some important philosopher questions!

Okay, time in.

Surely we haven't ruled out *all* possibilities when it comes to voting in an election. If we think about it, it should be obvious that we can't achieve the standard of absolute certainty for beliefs such as this. Even close personal friends of political candidates are sometimes surprised by things the candidates say into a hot mic or some recently unveiled secret about their past. The person we were so sure about turns out to be a fraud.

This doesn't mean we can't rationally and confidently believe that someone is the best candidate in an election. While we may not be able to have absolute certainty when it comes to who we should vote for, we can weigh the evidence and make up our minds in a rationally confident way. And this is the point. We should aim for rational confidence in these sorts of pursuits because certainty is a mere will-o'-the-wisp. Finite minds simply can't pull it off. Though the distinction between aiming at certainty and aiming at confidence is somewhat subtle, it makes a big difference.

Consider a few more beliefs:

- My airplane will arrive at its destination safely.
- Smith is guilty of the crime.
- I had toast with jam for breakfast today.

Can we have 100 percent certainty about any of these claims?

Though flying on airplanes is overall a safe mode of travel, too many things could go wrong to have 100 percent certainty. It doesn't matter how much research you do or how many times you have flown before. You can't rule out all those possibilities. If we had to rule out all possibilities, we would never get onboard another airplane. Does this make us irrational for flying? Of course not. Most of us have good and rational reasons to board with confidence and believe that we'll arrive safely at our destination.

How about "Smith is guilty of the crime"? Let's say there is considerable evidence presented against Smith in the trial, including eyewitness testimony that implicates him as guilty. Suppose it looks bad for Smith. Could we have certainty that Smith is guilty? No, not 100 percent certainty. It's happened many times that some new evidence will come along and completely exonerate someone who appeared guilty. This is why the standard of proof to convict is "believing beyond a reasonable doubt." If certainty was required (that is, believing beyond all *possible* doubt), then there would never be a conviction. Again, there will always be some possibility of doubt. While we may have our minds made up and be quite confident that Smith is guilty, we won't have certainty no matter how strong the evidence is.

Are you certain about what you had for breakfast this morning? Now it seems we can have a high level of confidence here. I may vividly remember having toast with jam. Even with this memory, it still seems quite possible (especially the older I get) I'm mixing up what I had for breakfast yesterday. It could be that yesterday I had toast with jam, and this morning I just had plain toast or skipped breakfast altogether. Let's be clear, we don't usually get the belief about what we had for breakfast wrong. However, the possibility remains.

Here's the point. We don't have absolute certainty so long as there is a mere possibility of being wrong. To admit this does not make us double-minded or wavering. This fact alone should not keep us from believing something with great confidence. Our reality is that for many of our common and everyday beliefs, we lack absolute certainty. There's always a chance we could be wrong.

Confidence in History and the Things People Say

How about other sorts of claims? Are you certain Julius Caesar crossed the Rubicon in 49 BC?

Okay, you maybe didn't even know the date of Caesar's crossing the Rubicon or even that Julius Caesar crossed this important river. But this is a well-known historical fact marking the beginning of Caesar's ascension as emperor. Could we know this historical fact with certainty? Clearly not! Even if we were a scholar of Roman history with a PhD in early Roman studies, we could have the date slightly wrong. This is because we are depending on records from that period, and these records could be inaccurate (even if slightly) for one reason or another. We have well worked out methods of historiography that make this claim rather likely, and so, again, we can have high confidence that it is true. But it falls far short of absolute certainty.

For another historical example, what happened on July 4, 1776? The United States voted to declare independence from Britain, right? Actually, no. That happened two days before, prompting founding father John Adams to say, "The Second Day of July 1776, will be the most memorable [day], in the History of America."[1] He was close. The day the Declaration of Independence was formally adopted, July 4, 1776, has become memorialized forevermore with fireworks, parades, camping, and cookouts.

Historical claims, by their very nature, cannot be known with certainty because there is always some possibility that the details of an event are not recorded accurately. Our memories are fallible. There's always a chance we misremember. And it is always possible we misperceive. Thus, there's always a chance that someone reports inaccurately, either intentionally or by mistake, even if they are very close to the events. This is true if it is testimony coming from a historical source, the testimony of our memories, or even the observation involved in scientific theorizing. Though some theories of science are claimed to be known with certainty, the reality is there is always some chance of error, even if ever so slight.

In Search of Certainty

In his *Meditations on First Philosophy*, René Descartes famously set out to find certainty. He does this because he is struck by the many falsehoods we accept from childhood. So, as a way to purify his knowledge, he decides to adopt a process of demolition. He plans, as he says, to "demolish everything completely and start again right from the foundations."[2] To do this, he will attempt to doubt all of his beliefs to find those which are indubitable (or undoubtable) and therefore certain. He plans to build back but only upon certainty.

To doubt everything Descartes subjects his beliefs to a few famous "thought experiments." He considers a series of possible (even if far-fetched) scenarios where his beliefs would be false. For example, he considers whether he could be dreaming right now and all of what he is experiencing would be a figment of his imagined dream experience. If we had an extraordinarily vivid dream, then much of what we believe we are experiencing would be false. You might think you are reading a book right now, but if you are dreaming, this would be false. You would be in your bed dreaming of reading a book.

The most powerful thought experiment that Descartes gives is one about a "malicious demon of the utmost power and cunning [who] has employed all of his energies to deceive."[3] Descartes imagines that this evil demon has the power to produce all our experiences. Everything that I am experiencing right now would be produced not by the objects I believe I am experiencing but by the demon's machinations. The demon is so powerful it can make our experiences—all our experiences—indistinguishable from experiencing the real thing. We often know we are dreaming (assuming we know when we wake up) because the dream seems qualitatively less real than our waking experiences.[4] So if the dream argument doesn't demolish all of our certainty, the evil demon argument seems to cast the possibility of doubt on *all* of my beliefs about my experiences.

But rather than despair, Descartes realizes that all is not lost. There's one thing he can have certainty about, and that's his existence. He can try to doubt his existence by saying "I doubt I exist." But this requires an *I* to do the doubting. This is meant to be something of an epiphany. Whenever I am thinking, whether it is doubting something or just holding an idea in thought, there is an *I* that's doing the doubting or the thinking. So, he claims [drum roll], "I think, therefore, I am." There is no possibility of this belief being false whenever he is thinking it. Upon this, Descartes attempts to continue to build back knowledge.

Many philosophers think that Descartes was right about "I think, therefore, I am." The fact that I exist can be known with certainty whenever I am thinking it. Descartes's project falls short, however, because "I think, therefore, I am" is simply too meager as a basis to build back all the things we take ourselves to know. I might know that I exist when I'm thinking about it, but I still don't have certainty that there's a book in front of me. He does a fantastic job of showing how few things we can be certain about. But if certainty is what we need, then there's very little we actually know.

The problem, it seems, is the starting place of certainty. Why think we have to be certain about the things we believe? We simply cannot meet this standard in so many of our beliefs. We can be certain about our existence. Okay, but what else? Philosophers also think simple facts of arithmetic and logical principles can be known with certainty. This is because these hold with logical necessity. Consider that 2+3=5. Ask yourself if it's possible that 2 added to 3 could equal something other than 5. It seems to many that you couldn't even imagine this possibility without changing the meanings of the terms.

Even if we are willing to grant that these can be known with certainty, we still would know very little about the world.

Is Christianity Possibly False?

Here comes the pressing question. Can we have certainty about Christianity, or is it also possibly false? I know, I know, it's another philosopher's question. And it may sound like I'm trying to undermine your faith. I'm not. This is a really important question to ask to understand how to approach our Christian claims.

Many Christians will be tempted to immediately say, no, Christianity is not possibly false. But let's be clear about what is being asked. To say that Christianity is possibly false does *not* mean that Christianity *is* false. It also does *not* mean that Christianity is *probably* false. It doesn't even mean that we are fifty-fifty on whether it is false or that we are concerned or worried about it being false. All that "being possibly false" means is that there is some chance, however slight, that Christianity is false.

As we've said, 2+3=5 is not possibly false, and the claim "I think, therefore, I am" is not possibly false. But when we ask if there is at least some chance that Christianity is false, in one important sense the answer is a clear yes. Once again, this doesn't mean it is actually false or even likely false. I believe it is true and I have given my life to its truth! But it is the kind of claim that is *possibly* false. The reason for this is that the truth of Christianity crucially depends on the claims of history, observation, and memory.

Resurrection Claims

Consider what Paul says in 1 Corinthians 15:13-19:

> If there is no resurrection of the dead, then not even Christ has been raised. And if Christ has not been raised, then our preaching is useless and so is your faith. . . . [Y]our faith is futile; you are still in your sins. . . . If only for this life we have hope in Christ, we are of all people most to be pitied.

Paul explicitly predicates Christianity on the truth of a historical event, namely, Jesus' resurrection. If this historical event did not take place, then our faith is in vain, worthless, and we should be pitied!

Now if it is all based on whether Jesus historically rose from the dead, then this makes the truth of Christianity turn on a historical claim, and historical claims can't be known with absolute certainty. As I said earlier, it is always possible that a historical event is reported inaccurately. If we ask ourselves if it is possible that Jesus did not rise from the dead, the answer should be in the clear affirmative. This isn't like doubting our own existence. It seems, at least, possible. In this passage Paul himself seems to be pondering the implications of this possibility. He says that if Jesus was not raised from the dead, then our faith is futile and held in vain.

This realization is so crucial because it shows that evidence is extremely important to holding the belief that Jesus was raised from the dead and consequently that Christianity is true. And if we back up in the passage even further, we see that Paul lays out a case for the resurrection. He identifies a variety of eyewitnesses to the risen Christ, including himself (1 Corinthians 15:5-8). The flow of the chapter is (1) he gives the gospel, which is predicated on the historicity of the resurrection of Jesus, (2) he gives a list of eyewitnesses for us to know that it happened, and (3) then says if this didn't happen, our faith is futile. Paul makes a rationally compelling case precisely because this is not a belief that can be held with absolute certainty.

Obviously, the apostle Paul doesn't think that Christianity is false or probably false. He's not fifty-fifty or wavering at all on Christianity! Paul believes in the resurrection with every ounce of his being. He has given his very life to it and demonstrates his confidence as he pays the ultimate price in martyrdom. Paul is convinced Christianity is true. But he is here referencing the mere possibility of our faith being in vain. He may be 100 percent confident that it is true, given, among other things, the eyewitness testimony he lists. But considering the nature of the claim, it is not something about which Paul can have 100 percent absolute certainty.

This might make us feel a bit uneasy, but it shouldn't. It's simply to say that many of the central claims of Christianity require evidence. If Christianity wasn't possibly false, then there would be no point in defending its truth. When it comes to an event like the resurrection, evidence matters. And here's the good news: the case for the resurrection is quite strong. I think it is so strong that I too have given my life to its truth, and so have many thoughtful Christians who have come before.

The Risk of Certainty

When we aim at certainty when it comes to our Christian beliefs, it sets us up for failure. When we think we have certainty for our beliefs and that nothing less will do, what happens when some hard challenge comes along? What happens when there is a question we can't fully answer? What happens if we are struggling with doubt? If we've made it all about certainty, then with a single unanswered question the whole thing comes crashing down.

Imagine someone with a lot of time on their hands who painstakingly constructs a five-foot-high house of cards. A house of cards is a structure of playing cards that are carefully leaned against and stacked on top of each other. That makes an impressive five feet of stacked cards. Here's the thing about a house of cards: it's necessarily precarious. Playing cards were never intended to be stacked and leaned against one another. When we see it, it's natural to wonder how it doesn't all fall down! And it will fall if someone removes or even just tweaks a single card. If we are committed to having certainty, then our faith is like this house of cards. All it takes is one question that we can't answer and we no longer have certainty. And the whole thing comes tumbling down.

We often set up our kids for failure when we tell them that they need to have absolute certainty that Christianity is true. If they should have certainty, they think, *Why do I have so many questions?* This is especially difficult when they arrive on a university campus where the smartest people around think Christianity is just a fairy tale and a fabrication. If it is so certain, then why do so many smart people disagree? Setting our sights on certainty sets up the Christian to fail when they inevitably find themselves with questions.

Here's the thing. I'm not a Christian because I am *certain* Christianity is true. I am a Christian because I am *confident* it is true. I'm not 100 percent certain (because this is impossible), but I am 100 percent confident. Confidence can withstand questions and challenges in a way certainty cannot. I can be completely confident that Christianity is true even if I have some unanswered questions and even if I'm facing challenges to my belief.

I can't be 100 percent certain that my flight will arrive safely, that Smith is guilty of the crime, or that I had toast with jam for breakfast. But I can be confident of these when I base my belief on good evidence. Instead of requiring absolute certainty, we should have a good reason for the things we believe.

In the same way, we can't have absolute certainty of the truth of Christianity. It is possible that Jesus did not rise from the dead. But, again, why do we think we need to have certainty in the first place? We want to aim instead at rational confidence in its truth and confidence to place our faith in him. How will we gain confidence? This comes from the investigation. As we ask the big questions leaning into our doubts and as we find answers, we grow in our confidence. And then confidence can stand strong as we encounter challenges.

Certainty That Christianity Is False?

There is a flip side to this. We may not have absolute certainty that Christianity is true, but it follows that we can't have absolute certainty that Christianity is false either. Many atheists seem to think they have certainty that God does not exist and that Christianity is false. On one side of things, we have Christian fundamentalists who allege to be certain about the truth of Christianity. On the other side, we have hardline skeptics who think there is no possible way Christianity (or any other religion) is true. Both mistakenly think they are in a place of certainty.

Some atheists have reported doubting their beliefs. C. S. Lewis reports having doubted his atheism before coming to the Christian faith. So did one of his students; Sheldon Vanauken, a student at Oxford University and friend of Lewis, described a moment of his journey this way:

> Christianity . . . seemed probable to me. But there is a gap between the probable and the proved. How was I to cross it? If I were to stake my whole life on the Risen Christ, I

wanted proof. I wanted certainty. I wanted to see Him eat a bit of fish. I wanted letters of fire across the sky. I got none of these. And I continued to hang about on the edge of the gap.[5]

The turning point for Vanauken came when he realized there was a gap with any choice he could make. He couldn't, given what he had come to know of Jesus, reasonably go back to his former ambivalence. And this was startling. He says,

My God! There was a gap behind me as well! Perhaps the leap to acceptance was a horrifying gamble—but what of the leap to rejection? There might be no certainty that Christ was God—but, by God, there was no certainty that he was not. This was not to be borne. I could not reject Jesus. There was only one thing to do once I had seen the gap behind me. I turned away from it, and flung myself over the gap towards Jesus.[6]

Vanauken realizes that requiring certainty was a distinct problem. He saw the good reason to believe that Christianity is true, but he didn't have absolute certainty. He thought he needed certainty, except that this proved impossible no matter what position he held. He came to realize there is no certainty in not committing to Christianity either. There was a gap in both directions. The less promising gap was the one he would have to leap to reject Christianity.

Intellectual Humility

The point is not to encourage you to struggle in your faith but to be honest and clear about the truth status of Christianity.

Faith, when understood properly, can tolerate big questions and significant doubts. Faith, when understood as requiring certainty, can't tolerate any question or doubt whatsoever. We should have questions, and many of us are going to doubt along the way. There is no biblical expectation that we have absolute certainty. In fact, the Bible characterizes our knowledge as limited. Paul says, "For now we see in a mirror dimly, but then face to face; now I know in part, but then I will know fully, just as I also have been fully known" (1 Corinthians 13:12 NASB). He contrasts our knowledge situation now compared to how it will be in the end.

At best we see reality dimly and know in part. The passage is clear that we *do* see and we *do* know, but we are a long shot from perfect knowledge. We only see the things dimly and in part. This is why we need to ask the big questions. But it's also why some of our questions will go unanswered and doubts may creep in. I, along with Paul, suggest we can know, even if imperfectly, and we can have complete confidence that Christianity is true. But that's going to take a confrontation with the evidence.

The Virtue of Faith

Faith does not eliminate questions.
But faith knows where to take them.

ELISABETH ELLIOT

Faith and reason are like two wings on which the human spirit
rises to the contemplation of truth; and God has placed in
the human heart a desire to know the truth—in a word,
to know himself—so that, by knowing and loving God,
men and women may also come to the fulness of
truth about themselves.

POPE JOHN PAUL II

There is perhaps no notion more important to the Christian life than faith. But at the same time there is perhaps no term more misunderstood. If you were to ask someone to define *faith*, they would not likely have a careful definition in their back pocket. Maybe they would identify it with belief or trust, or maybe they would quote a Bible passage, such as Hebrews 11:1. But, more than likely, they will just say, "It's just . . . it's just faith." For many Christians it's the secret sauce of Christianity in that there's nothing more important for us to cultivate, but we don't seem to know what it is. It's seen as something mysterious that sort of just happens at altar calls, gospel invitations, and quiet moments of prayer.

Faith Versus Belief

There's no shortage of the religiously faithless who seem eager to tell us what faith is. Many of these characterizations of faith are reminiscent of Mark Twain's precocious schoolboy who quipped, "Faith is believing what you know ain't so."[1] The figurehead of the so-called New Atheist movement, Richard Dawkins, once said, "Faith is belief in spite of, even perhaps because of, the lack of evidence."[2] His colleague Sam Harris puts it this way: "Faith is nothing more than the license religious people give one another to keep believing when reasons fail."[3] The most obnoxious characterization of faith comes from Peter Boghossian, who thinks faith is a virus, a kind of mental health issue, that needs to be eradicated. He characterizes faith as "pretending to know things that you don't know" and the slightly—but only slightly—more charitable "belief without evidence."[4]

Unfortunately, exactly none of these engage what Christian thinkers have said about faith. At best they offer anecdotes about what religious people have said along the way. But this is not the way to do serious thinking on a topic. And these caricatures of faith seem designed to be easily defeated. If you are in a rational debate about faith with a critic of faith and the critic gets you to agree that faith is belief without evidence, then this is checkmate. The contest is over. You've just agreed that faith isn't rational, and so by definition you've lost the (rational) debate.

The problem is that there are well-meaning Christians who, especially when backed into a corner, are willing to affirm notions of faith similar to these. Here's how the conversation often goes:

CRITIC   Why do you believe that Christianity is true?

CHRISTIAN   There's just sooo much evidence.

CRITIC   Okay, what is some of it?

CHRISTIAN   Well, um, uh, I think I wrote it down somewhere.

CRITIC   Isn't it a problem that you can't remember any of the evidence?

CHRISTIAN   No, not really. I just have faith.

Christians sometimes talk as if faith is something like belief without evidence.

But there's an important mistake in all of this. The mistake is thinking that faith is some sort of belief or way of knowing—and for the critic it's thought to be a bad kind of belief and a flawed way of knowing. There may be many beliefs we embrace on the way to faith, and perhaps we need to know some things to know where we should place our faith. Even so, faith itself is not in the belief or knowledge category. It's in the category of trust and action.

We see this mistake in the definitions of faith listed earlier. Each of them understands faith as a belief or way of knowing. Take, for example, the idea that faith is belief without evidence. Notice this view sees faith as a certain kind of *belief* and a certain kind of bad belief at that. But why think faith is a belief to start with? That is, why think it is a mere intellectual commitment? My claim is that faith is not a bad belief because it is not a belief at all. It is not a flawed way of knowing because it is not itself a way of knowing. Instead, faith is an act of trust.

Suppose I believe the airplane I'm about to board is safe. Suppose I even *know* that the airplane is safe. But I don't place my faith in the airplane until the moment I get on board. Faith is a step further. It's an act of trust.

Believing That and Believing In

One question that may be raised is why the Bible talks so much about belief if belief and faith are not the same thing. Take for example the most famous verse in the Bible: "For God so loved the world that he gave his one and only Son, that whoever believes in him shall not perish but have eternal life" (John 3:16). Doesn't this verse tell us that if we believe, then we will have eternal life? How does faith fit into this?

Though the word used here is *belief*, I think it's safe to assume Jesus doesn't mean mere intellectual assent. When we look at the ministry of Jesus, he wasn't so much interested in mere intellectual commitments as he was in commitments of trust. It's not as if all we must do is intellectually believe that Jesus died on the cross and rose from the dead and then we'll have eternal life. We can intellectually believe something and it makes no difference in our life. Beliefs are important, but Jesus was all about our commitments and life change.

Notice the construction in John 3:16 is to "believe *in*" the Son and not believe *that* certain things are the case. In the context of the passage Nicodemus already admits to knowing *that* Jesus has come from God (John 3:2). But Jesus calls him to something further. He calls him to a place of faith in believing *in* him. The Bible of course calls us to intellectually believe certain theological claims as well. However, the point here is that faith is not mere belief; it is something beyond mere belief. Believing *in* Jesus is trusting him as his follower.

In James 2, James makes a striking claim. In the passage, he's contrasting someone who merely claims to have faith with a faith that is lived out. He goes on to say, "You believe that there is one God. Good! Even the demons believe that—and shudder" (v. 19).

What's striking about this passage, especially if you've never thought about it before, is that the demons have a variety of Christian beliefs! And they are not happy about it. But even with theologically correct beliefs, they lack faith. They are not followers of the Christian way.

To see this distinction a bit more crisply, suppose I have never bungee jumped before. Suppose I know almost nothing about bungee jumping. I don't know what it is. I haven't researched it and I don't know anyone who has bungee jumped before. I'm not likely to take the jump until I believe that bungee jumping is safe. But let's say I get those reasons and I come to believe it's safe. In this case I believe *that* bungee jumping is safe, but I haven't believed *in* (i.e., placed my faith in) the bungee.

But let's say I decide I am going to jump. Notice my intellectual commitments haven't changed. I still believe that bungee jumping is a safe activity. Something else has changed. I've made a decision to *trust in action*. The moment I jump is the moment I have faith.

This isn't to say that beliefs are unimportant for placing faith. Faith typically follows what we believe or know to be the case. Notice I'm not likely to jump until I know a few things about bungee jumping and its safety. We don't typically place our faith in something we believe is unsafe or that doesn't exist. But faith is a step further from mere intellectual commitment.

What Then Is Faith?

If faith is not itself a belief, what is this thing we call faith? Faith is most fundamentally an attitude of trust and dependence. J. P. Moreland says, "Faith is relying on what you have reason to believe is true and trustworthy."[5] When we trust, there is always a thing or person we trust. This could be the bungee cord that's strapped to our ankles, a chair we sit in, an airplane we are boarding, or a person to whom we say "I do." When we place faith in someone or something, we act in trust.

On this way of understanding faith, we can't have faith from a distance. Faith is *trust in action*. Placing faith in the bungee cord requires us to jump and entrust ourselves to it. We have faith the moment we jump. In this way we always *venture* on someone or something when we place faith. Faith requires not trust from a distance but rather entrusting ourselves where we venture or risk ourselves and our well-being on that person or thing.

There is then something of a leap. And as I'll say below, it shouldn't be a blind leap. We should only trust on the basis of good reasons. So you ought to know something about the safety of bungee jumping and inspect the bungee cord, platform, and so on, before you jump. But the point is, to place faith in the bungee cord, we still have to leap and venture ourselves on it. In other instances of faith, it may be a relatively small venture as we, say, sit in a chair. The chair may collapse. It's a small risk, but still a risk. But it may be we risk our very lives as we leap hundreds of feet venturing on a bungee cord strapped to our ankles.

Similarly, we risk ourselves when we place our faith in a person. When we place faith in a person, we risk that person letting us down. A child is often completely dependent on their parent for their well-being. A withdrawn or abusive parent can create lifelong harm in a child precisely because the child places trust in the parent.

Marriage is another great venture. A healthy marriage requires us to entrust virtually every area of our lives to our spouse, and this opens us up to the possibility of the deepest hurt when there is betrayal. A toxic marriage is, of course, when there is deep distrust and suspicion. It can be very difficult to get over an act of betrayal in a marriage. But a marriage won't be healthy unless each spouse can take the risk of venturing trust. Indeed a healthy marriage requires us to fully jump in with deep and mutual ventured trust.

With this understanding of faith, everyone, including the most radically committed atheist, has faith insofar as they entrust themselves to someone or something. Presumably, they too sit in chairs, fly on airplanes, and have deep relationships. Maybe they've even bungee jumped. Even in our most academic pursuits we place faith. The most rationalistic scientist trusts certain methods, colleagues, prior theories and data, and empirical and mental faculties. A person may not have a religious faith, of course, but we can't survive without placing our trust in a variety of things and people.

Virtues and Vices

With this understanding of faith as ventured trust, we can see that faith can be good, perhaps even virtuous, or it can be misapplied. This is to say we can place our faith in the right sorts of things or the wrong ones.

Suppose your college friend invites you on a cross-country road trip. So, up for the adventure, you pack a bag and excitedly haul it down to the parking lot—and there you see it. Your buddy pulls in with a sorry excuse for an automobile: rusted, backfiring, smoking, and leaking fluids. You are not entirely sure it will even start again, much less make it across the country! Here's the question: Could you place your faith in this vehicle? Could you venture your trust in it? Yes. You could jump in and take off down the road (assuming it starts). Now the problem is you'll likely end up on the side of the road in the not-too-distant future. But here's a different question: *Should* you place your faith in this vehicle? Would it be good to do so? Here the answer is a decisive no. It seems it would be a very bad idea and irresponsible to place faith in that vehicle.

This example illustrates nicely the role reason should play when it comes to faith. It would be bad to place your faith in this vehicle precisely because you have obvious reasons that count against doing so. Could you do it? Yes. But you shouldn't. When you inspect it, you find more than a few red flags. If, on the other hand, it is a relatively new car, in good shape, and recently serviced, then you have good reason to trust it. *Reasons* are informing what is a worthy object of faith. We want something that is trustworthy—or what we may call *faith-worthy*—and reason and evidence help us know what things to trust and what things not to trust. How else would we know in what or in whom to place our trust? The history of the debate about the relationship of faith and reason is long, but we need not make it overly complicated. Reason is simply a tool to help us know what or who to place our faith in.

Virtuous Faith

Faith is good when we have good reasons and evidence for placing our faith in that person or thing. This is *virtuous faith*. We can't get along well without it. We need to place our trust in things to get along in life. Most of us need a good car or some reliable means of transportation, without it our pursuits will be frustrated.

More importantly we need good and faithful people in our lives who we can reasonably trust. Without dependable people, life would be extremely difficult to navigate. If we continually place our faith in people who double-cross, manipulate, and harm us, we will not flourish in life.

How do we know a person is faith-worthy? In some ways, knowing whether a car is faith-worthy is straightforward. So long as we have evidence the thing functions the way we want it to, then it is a faith-worthy object. When it comes to a person, things are a bit different. People have intentions, a will, and sometimes hidden purposes in their actions. People can function a certain way at one moment and then stab you in the back the next! To know that a person is faith-worthy we need to know the person is both competent and a friend. Let me explain.

In an age of Facebook and other social media channels, the notion of a friend has been watered down considerably. Aristotle once said, "To be friends . . . two [people] should be well-disposed towards each other and wish each other's good without being unaware of this."[6] Is a person you hang out with a friend? Well, according to Aristotle, it depends on whether they are well-intentioned toward you and you are aware of this. Does the person have your well-being in mind in the relationship? If we have seen evidence of this, then it seems we have reason to trust that person. This is for the rather obvious reason that it is a bad idea to entrust ourselves to people who do not have our well-being as their interest or aim. In short, we should only place our faith in someone who is a genuine friend.

But being a friend isn't quite all there is to it. We've probably known people who mean well and sincerely love us but for some reason disaster always follows them. In addition to knowing that someone is a friend, we need to know they are also competent at being a friend. We shouldn't, it seems, trust an incompetent person even if the person is well-intentioned. Take, for example, someone who has proposed a joint business venture with you. Now this person is a friend and means well. However, the problem, let's say, is this person unintentionally makes terrible business decisions regularly, ones that often result in disaster. Even though he may be a friend, I'd suggest not entering into a business deal with this person.

Putting this together, if someone is a competent friend, then this person is faith-worthy. The question is, how do we know when someone is a genuine friend who is competent. What constitutes evidence of a competent friend? Again, it's painfully obvious that we can, at times, be wrong about these things in our relationships. However, it is also clear that we can exercise due care and have the right people in our lives.

A genuine friend is one who comes through for us and self-sacrificially meets our needs. A person who is unwilling to even suffer a mere inconvenience on our behalf is not a great friend. Or a person who cannot come through for us isn't someone we place our trust in. We of course can never know with certainty that someone has our interest in mind or that they'll come through for us (this is why all friendships come with risk), but we can see behavior that is best explained by a friend's having a good will toward us in competent ways. In our time of need, a genuine friend will stand by us, helping us get through no matter the inconvenience or sacrifice.

It seems the ultimate evidence that someone is a friend is that person's willingness to give their life for the other. Jesus himself said, "Greater love has no one than this: to lay down one's life for one's friends" (John 15:13). It is easy to *say* we will give our life, but doing so is another matter entirely. This is of course the ultimate proof that someone is a genuine friend deserving of our full trust.

Christian Faith

We have in Christianity the claim that God, the omnipotently competent one, loves us and gave his Son for us. If this is true, then this certainly calls for a response of venturing our lives on him. Here again, we need reasons to believe that this sort of God is there and has these intentions toward us. We are not called to a blind leap. The evidence matters. Is there significant evidence for the Christian claim? Yes, and we'll get there soon enough in subsequent chapters. For now, we should understand, on the Christian view, we are called to faith precisely because the central claim of the gospel is that Jesus, in his great love for us and despite our sin, gave his life for us, making a way to God. But this isn't the end of the story. Jesus defeated death in the resurrection, and in this we too may live life eternal. There's no greater act of self-sacrifice and love in all of human history than this!

In this we have an ultimately worthy object of our faith, namely, the triune God of the Christian Bible. If we have evidence that God is there and that he is maximally great and perfect in all of his ways, and we have reason to believe that God loves us and gave his Son for us, then we know he's the greatest possible friend. And this calls for faith. Coming to a place of confidence in the reality of these facts makes our faith well-grounded.

Faith Seeking Understanding

Emphasizing the importance of evidence has the danger of sounding as if this is a completely intellectual exercise. We are far more than mere thinking things. As we'll see in chapter nine, the Christian gospel is not just reasonable, but it also satisfies our deepest longings.

We are also not going to get it all figured out in an investigation beforehand. Saint Anselm of Canterbury stressed that we approach God with faith seeking understanding (*fides quaerens intellectum*). While I'm convinced that evidence matters, we do need to, at some point, place faith. The idea is that starting the journey of faith actually brings a greater and deeper understanding. If we try to work it all out beforehand and never place faith in God, we will only ever have a limited understanding.

I can research all there is to know about bungee jumping. But I won't understand it—really and fully understand it—until I take my first jump. We can study the statistics about how safe rappelling down a rock face is. But at some point, I need to put some weight on the ropes. I need to start inching my way down and, as I do, I'll understand more and more. Once my feet hit the bottom, I understand the trustworthiness of the ropes in ways I couldn't at the top of the rock face. I knew much *about* my wife when we were dating and engaged. But it wasn't until we joined our lives together and I navigated life alongside her, entrusting myself to her, that I really understood who she is and her extreme faith-worthiness.

No one comes to faith having it all figured out. There comes a time to leap even though we still may have some questions and some doubts. Once again, this need not be a blind and irrational leap. We often need a few questions answered before we are ready to take this leap. But at some point we should venture trust. We should begin the journey of faith. Questioning doesn't stop. As we walk, intentionally wandering toward God, we should seek greater understanding. In this, God shows up in our lives. Jesus says, "Seek and you will find. . . . The one who seeks finds" (Matthew 7:7-8). As we seek him on the journey of faith we'll see God clearer, and in our knowledge of him we trust him more confidently.

Doubt Your Doubts

Knowledge grows not only by doubting your beliefs and believing your doubts, but by doubting your doubts and believing your beliefs.

DALLAS WILLARD

The relationship between commitment and doubt is by no means an antagonistic one. Commitment is healthiest when it is not without doubt but in spite of doubt.

ROLLO MAY

When we are seeking to understand something as big as God, it's normal to have doubts along the way. We don't typically have much choice in whether we struggle with some doubts in this process, but we do make choices in how to deal with the doubt. My claim is that doubt, when handled properly, leads to truth. Even if it turns out that we change our beliefs, we have presumably come to a more rational place as a result of the doubts. But if Christianity is true, as we lean in and find answers to our questions we grow in our knowledge and come to a place of even greater faith. Let's talk about how to handle doubt properly.

Being Beat Up by Doubt

When you doubt your faith, you often feel like you've been beat up. It's not usually fun to feel like one of your beliefs might be false, especially when it's one of your cherished beliefs. This can be a lonely place. Sometimes it feels like you have stumbled on something people either have never seen or are just ignoring. You wonder why no one else is talking about the issue you've found. What adds to the isolation is you might be brave enough to share your doubts with another Christian only to have that person dismiss your doubts as insignificant. Too often when it comes to doubting, pastors and well-meaning Christians are telling people to, in effect, knock it off, as if doubting is nothing more than a bad choice we are making.

Here's a ticking time bomb: you have some questions, and these questions are causing you to doubt, but you can't find a safe place to address those doubts. If you've also been told by your pastor or a parent that faith requires absolute certainty and anything short of that is sin, you will find yourself in what may feel like a hopeless struggle. Since no one is willing to take the time and effort to provide answers to your questions, it can feel like there are no answers.

The great shame is this couldn't be further from the truth. When it comes to questioning Christianity, there's nothing new under the sun. We stand in a long tradition of Christians asking deep and difficult questions and pressing Christianity for its truth. Consequently, virtually every question we may have has been asked in one form or fashion at some point. It might feel like you've discovered something brand new. But chances are excellent that it's been at least thoughtfully addressed by someone at some point.

This is not to make light of the questions you have. I, in fact, want you to take your questions very seriously. But just don't let them have their way with you. And don't give in to the feelings of isolation. You are not alone. There are a lot of us out there. Chances are others have wrestled with the very same questions you have, and you should have a careful look at what they say.

Early on, it was so helpful to know there were those much further down the road from me who had long grappled with the hardest objections to Christian faith and still believed. In all humility, may I be that to you as you walk this journey? I've been working on these issues for over twenty years now and have tried my best to confront every objection I find. I've also tried to be as brutally honest as I can. So far, I haven't found the smoking gun that shows Christianity false. I still have questions, but I don't know of a serious objection to Christianity that doesn't have a significant literature of thoughtful Christians offering thoughtful answers, many of which I find compelling. I still find the Christian view to have, on balance, the best answers to life's biggest questions.

Bumper Sticker Theology

Unfortunately Christians sometimes act like there are no challenges to Christianity. They go with the mentality of the bumper sticker that says "God said it. I believe it. That settles it." Now, this saying is not *completely* wrong. If you know God said something, then that's really good reason to believe it, and this should settle the issue. But we of course have to first *know* that God said it. It may be the case that something is clearly stated in Scripture, but this doesn't help settle it for someone who is struggling with whether to believe the words of Scripture. Saying "just believe it" is simply not helpful here.

This "just believe it" mentality has another very serious issue as it relates to leading our kids to faith. If every time my child has a question or a struggle and I always say "just believe it," if I don't ever give them reasons to believe, then I train my kid to unquestioningly follow me as the authority in their life. If this is all we ever do, our kids don't learn to think for themselves since, after all, they are supposed to just believe it.

But there will come a time (let's all hope) when the kids get out of the house. What happens if they find themselves in, say, a class on a secular campus with a smart and winsome professor offering arguments against Christian beliefs? If we haven't taught our kids to think critically about challenges, then guess who becomes the new authority in their life? Why would we think they'd question their new authorities if they haven't questioned and thought critically about their Christian beliefs? We have taught them to "just believe it."

What's worse is we miss the opportunity that doubt provides. This is going to sound provocative, but I want my kids to question their faith. This may lead them to doubt their faith a bit. Now this may be a bit gut wrenching to watch them go through. But doubting their faith provides an opportunity for me to come alongside my kids and help them find the truth. I would much rather that happens in my home and not on a university campus that's entirely hostile to faith.

I would much rather have them ask me deep and difficult questions about their faith and wrestle with it along the way before they have a professor or a roommate or office co-worker challenging them with hard questions. By the time they get into those settings, I want the hard-hitting objections to feel familiar.

John the Baptist Has a Question

Besides Jesus, perhaps the figure held in the highest regard in the Gospels is John the Baptist. Jesus himself said, "Truly I tell you, among those born of women there has not risen anyone greater than John the Baptist" (Matthew 11:11). John the Baptist is an enigmatic figure in the Bible. He preaches in the desert as a kind of wild but righteous man. He very literally starts the movement that Jesus comes to spearhead. People come in droves to the desert to be baptized by John. Jesus himself comes to the desert, and John reluctantly baptizes him.

When Jesus comes on the scene, John immediately recognizes Jesus as the "Lamb of God" (John 1:29, 36), a clear recognition of Jesus as the Jewish Messiah promised throughout the Old Testament. As Jesus is baptized, God speaks and says, "This is my Son, whom I love; with him I am well pleased" (Matthew 3:17). John testifies that in this baptism experience he saw the Spirit of God coming down out of heaven like a dove upon Jesus and that this was a clear indication that Jesus is "God's Chosen One" (John 1:34), again a messianic reference.

But something changed in John the Baptist's thinking. This paragon of faith, who had clarity about who Jesus is, came to wonder about Jesus. John sent his disciples to Jesus to ask, "Are you the one who is to come, or should we expect someone else?" (Luke 7:20). John is, in effect, asking whether Jesus is the promised Messiah.

What happened? Well, by this point, John is in prison. He publicly criticized Herod, Rome's puppet king of the region of Judea, and for this John was thrown into prison. Did this perhaps cause him to wonder whether Jesus is the promised Messiah? The expected Messiah was supposed to free Israel from bondage and lead them to a place of ascendency on the world stage. But Israel remains occupied by Rome, and John, the Messiah's forerunner, is languishing in a Roman prison cell not knowing whether he will live or die. Jesus, meanwhile, is still just preaching in the desert. The political movement has not been organized, and there's no uprising on the horizon.

Perhaps thoughts such as these led John to question whether Jesus was the promised Messiah despite his earlier conviction. He felt confident in who he took Jesus to be, but now he's not so sure. In any case, whatever is going on in his mind, John the Baptist now has a big question.

Notice here that Jesus does not rebuke John for this question. He does not chide him saying "Ye of little faith." John the Baptist's question seems to be received as an honest question. But interestingly, Jesus answers the question by pointing to his miraculous works. He says to tell John, "The blind receive sight, the lame walk, those with leprosy are cleansed, the deaf hear, the dead are raised, and the good news is proclaimed to the poor" (Matthew 11:5). Now just like many things Jesus says, this has layers to it. Jesus tells John's disciples to report to John the life-changing miracles they have seen Jesus perform. But it's also a reference to Isaiah 35:5-6, which John would have known as a messianic passage. This is all to say to John loud and clear that Jesus is indeed "the One."

Evidence Matters

One takeaway here from John the Baptist's question is that the evidence matters. Jesus doesn't tell John to stop asking questions and just believe. He points to evidence of who he is. Jesus performed signs and wonders in clear view of people. He often avoided spectacle, but he didn't shy away from demonstrating who he was for those who were genuinely seeking.

This sort of evidence was certainly instrumental in the lives of Jesus' disciples. From seeing signs and wonders, their understanding of Jesus greatly expanded. After Jesus calms a violent storm, his disciples remark, "What kind of man is this? Even the winds and the waves obey him!" (Matthew 8:27). Jesus convinces Paul by appearing to him with blinding light and speaking to him on the road to Damascus (Acts 9:1-9). Now, we may not have direct experiences of Jesus in the same way as these. The point is that for Jesus to point to his miracles as evidence shows that evidence matters for our Christian beliefs.

When we ask deep and difficult questions, it's important to also look to the evidence. Again, this doesn't mean we'll get all of our questions answered thoroughly with irrefutable evidence. And it doesn't mean we won't experience doubt along the way. But, aiming at confidence, we should believe on the basis of good reasons. As we will discuss in subsequent chapters, there are many compelling arguments and evidence of all sorts (scientific, archaeological, historical, philosophical, and the like). I will also argue that Christian claims are the best explanation for reality as we find it.

Evidence matters because we ought to believe something because it's true. Christianity is not true *because* I believe it. I should believe it because I have found it to be true. This might sound a bit obvious, but the reason I doubted my faith in seminary was because I suddenly realized I lacked good reasons for my Christian beliefs. It was clear to me that the primary reason I believed was because I grew up in a Christian home. I realized I was a Christian by accident of my birth. This is why I had to look carefully at the evidence since, in that moment, I genuinely didn't know whether Christianity was true. With as honest a consideration as I could marshal, I found the evidence for Christianity compelling. The point is that we should believe because we have good and compelling reasons to take it to be true.

The Christian gospel is much more than merely true. It's good, beautiful, and transforming for all who are affected by it. But in a fundamental sense we need to come to see that it's true. If this is right, then this should shape how we approach our Christian faith and especially our doubts. We are going to ask big questions and follow the evidence where it leads. As we doubt, we need to also ask questions of the doubts as we press them for their truth. In short, we need to investigate our doubts.

How to Deal with Doubt

How then do we deal with doubt? Let's remind ourselves that doubt is an opportunity for greater depth. Though it is not an altogether enjoyable experience, there's value in leaning in and investigating our doubts. To do this well, I suggest two things.

Hang on! The first suggestion is to take a deep breath and hang on to our beliefs. Now this might be a bit surprising since I just said we are going to lean in and investigate our doubts. We will indeed lean in to our doubts. However, we don't want to lean in when the situation is overly pressurized. I don't mean to say that we should hang on to our beliefs no matter what. But we shouldn't let doubts have their way with us either. We need to take a deep breath and get a little emotional distance from the doubt, so we can consider with due care.

The reason we can do this is, again, the mere existence of doubt does not automatically defeat our Christian beliefs. They are simply part of the deal when we consider ideas honestly. It is normal to find some ideas, even ideas that we do not ultimately believe, somewhat plausible. That is, if we are asking good questions, then we will almost certainly feel some intellectual tension along the way. We should hang on precisely because this is a normal part of the process.

This is especially the case when we first encounter an idea and it is presented compellingly. But a claim that seems initially plausible is not necessarily a reasonable claim and thus not one that should defeat our Christian beliefs. Again, think of the last time a really good salesperson made a product seem amazing even though the product turned out to be inferior. You might have found the sales pitch unassailable, at first. You can't help but think, *I guess I can't live without this!* But let's be honest, it is not always reasonable. Often the best thing to do with a compelling sales pitch on an unplanned purchase is to take a deep breath (and maybe even sleep on it). Get some emotional distance from the pitch and see if it remains compelling. Products that might seem compelling in the heat of the moment often do not fulfill the grand promises of the sales pitch. In the same way that it is often helpful to pause before making an unplanned purchase, it is helpful to pause before conceding an objection that seems, in the moment, to be compelling.

And remember, it is perfectly rational to maintain our Christian faith while we have questions even if we are in the throes of doubt. Remember the analogy in chapter one of getting on an airplane even though we had some significant questions we couldn't answer. The image to have in mind is that we can be sitting on the airplane questioning how flight is even possible. We can do that while flying at six miles off the surface of the planet! It would be crazy to suddenly have some intellectual tension from an unanswered question and therefore jump out of the airplane. Well, I think it'd be equally crazy to reject our faith just because we have some intellectual tension. There are times to jump out of an airplane, and there are times to walk away from a cherished belief, but not merely because of the presence of questions and doubt.

A final reason to hang on is that I'm convinced that most Christians have sufficiently good reasons to hang on to faith. But we need to clarify what it means to have good reasons.

Having sufficiently good reason doesn't mean you can lay out a highly academic case that convinces all unbelieving people—or even a single unbelieving person, for that matter.

Being reasonable does not, in any way, turn on having well worked out academic reasons or being able to convince someone else. As long as you have reasons for taking Christianity to be true, you are (to some extent) rational even if one can't articulate those reasons.

In fact we often have far more reasons for our beliefs—especially important beliefs—than we are ever able to articulate. Suppose someone came up to me and asked for a compelling case for why flying on airplanes is safe. Probably the best I can do is say I know many people who fly, and I have flown in the past. I don't know, off the top of my head, any studies to cite or data referencing reliability. If I thought about it some more, I might remember that the FAA regulates air travel, which helps us know it's safe. But that's about all I've got on that. Is this going to be convincing to someone who is seriously skeptical about flying? Not likely. But, given my past experiences and what I do know, I do have sufficiently good reasons to get on board.

Or if someone demanded that I lay out a case for why I love my wife. I think I'd be able to articulate quite a few reasons, but there's a good chance that, on the spot, what I articulate wouldn't do justice to all the reasons I have from our twenty-year relationship. Some of the reasons are far too subtle to put into words (this is why Hallmark cards and love songs can be greatly helpful!). From the fact that I fail to articulate those reasons, it doesn't follow that those reasons aren't there.

Likewise, when Christians are put on the spot to lay out a case for Christianity, they may not articulate it well. But they likely have far more reasons than they realize. All of us came to our Christian beliefs for some reason or other. Again, it may not have been anything academic or too carefully thought out. It may have been that someone shared a powerful testimony about how the gospel changed their life. Or perhaps one has had extraordinary answers to prayer and seen God at work. These are good reasons and could have been what compelled us to believe.

Now, we can all improve the reasons we have for our beliefs. But for many, the Christian story makes good sense of reality as we find it. We all experience an exquisitely ordered universe that begs to be explained by a designing Creator. This is also a moral world. People have certain inalienable rights, and there are things that are objectively right and wrong. This is tough to explain if there is no God. We have also all experienced deep longings for the transcendent, and it's clear that nothing in this world fully satisfies. The gospel addresses these deep longings and points us to a divine fulfillment. Perhaps the best reason of all is that you have experienced the living God for yourself as he's convicted your heart and made himself real to you. If so, all of these constitute reasons for thinking that Christianity is true.

The point is, we should hang on in faith because most of us have at least *some* good reasons to believe even though we find ourselves with some doubts. If we jumped ship because of the mere presence of a doubt, then we would be like that doubter described by James—the one who is "like a wave of the sea, blown and tossed by the wind. . . . Such a person is double-minded and unstable in all they do" (James 1:6, 8).

So hang on! Don't jump out of the airplane just yet.

Doubt your doubts. So we have some doubts. We are going to hang on and first take a deep breath. After that, we investigate. Doubt, as I've defined it, is when a belief seems as if it might be false. Or the flipside is when an objection to one of our beliefs seems plausible. But changing our mind merely because it seems that a belief might be false or because an objection seems plausible without investigating its truth is irresponsible. Our doubts signal to us that something may be amiss. But the signal is for us to take a deeper look. It's the evidence over and above the mere seeming state that shows us if something is truly amiss. And an objection only defeats a belief when the evidence for it outweighs the evidence we have for our belief.

How do we investigate? I suggest we question our doubts—here we are doubting our doubts—to see whether there is good reason to think the doubts are sufficiently reasonable to outweigh the evidence we have for our beliefs.

As we investigate, we should ask two questions. First, "What's the problem?" Second, "Why think this claim is true?" Let's take each of these in turn.[1]

What's the Problem?

This first question is designed to determine whether the objection we find plausible is genuinely a problem. This is where we ask, "So what? What's the problem?" We are aiming to take stock of whether it is a problem and if so, how difficult the problem is. Many ideas seem problematic at first glance but turn out, on further reflection, to be completely benign.

Suppose that Smith believes that the Bible is without error. One day, his coworker asserts the idea that there are lots of errors throughout the Bible and points out the following passages. Each of these passages describes the same event, namely the empty tomb of Jesus, but all differ in who first witnessed it empty.

- Matthew says, "Mary Magdalene and the other Mary went to look at the tomb." (Matthew 28:1)
- Mark says, "Mary Magdalene, Mary the mother of James, and Salome . . . were on their way to the tomb." (Mark 16:1-2)
- Luke says, "It was Mary Magdalene, Joanna, Mary the mother of James, and the others with them . . ." (Luke 24:10)
- John says, "While it was still dark, Mary Magdalene went to the tomb." (John 20:1)

Suppose Smith has never noticed how different these passages are. We can imagine this could be extremely concerning. Let's say, on the basis of this challenge, he begins to find plausible the idea that these passages do contradict each other and that there must be errors here. That is, it seems his belief (that the Bible is without errors) might be false. Smith is doubting.

But now Smith is going to doubt his doubt. He asks, "What's the problem?" Each of these passages differs in who witnessed the empty tomb, but are these differences really a problem?

What we should notice is that differences of detail do not necessarily entail a contradiction. In fact, when we look at each account, none of them directly contradicts the others. They each affirm Mary Magdalene. While John only mentions Mary Magdalene, he doesn't say that Mary Magdalene went alone. Saying Mary was there in one account is consistent with saying Mary and Salome were there in another. If it is the case that a group of women were present at the empty tomb and that each account gives at least partial view of who was there, these are consistent (i.e., noncontradictory) accounts.

For an illustration of this, let's say to my great surprise the president of the United States, three of his aides, and his security detail showed up at my office one day. After they leave, I walk out of my office and see a coworker. I might blurt out "The president of the United States just came to my office!" Later, my wife wants to hear every last detail, and in this account I say, "There was the president, three of his aides, and his security detail all crammed into my office." Notice there are significantly different details in the two accounts, but I'm not lying or misrepresenting the details. There's no error here. I'm just choosing to highlight different details depending on who I'm talking to.

And as it turns out, differences of details are actually a good thing (so long as they are not contradictory) because they suggest multiple independent witnesses represented by the accounts. Different people will almost certainly emphasize different details in a single event. This is because a witness describes the situation from their vantage point, and no two vantage points are the same. Differences of detail are only a problem when the differences are unable to be reconciled, especially in the crucial details.

So having four different accounts implies we have four *independent* accounts. This makes for a stronger case because having four witnesses saying the same basic thing (that the tomb was empty) despite the differences of detail is stronger than having just one witness whose story is repeated four times with no differences of detail.

When we ask, "What's the problem?" we see that the mere fact that there are differences can be accounted for. There's not a real problem here. Now, not everything turns out as well as it does in this example. In my journey, the most common experience has been that when I've struggled with what seems like a significant problem for my Christian faith, as I leaned in, I have found answers that are more or less satisfying. Sometimes the problem goes away completely as in our example above. Other times, the answers are helpful and something of a start of a good answer, but the problem is still a concern. But again, what I haven't found is a smoking-gun objection that doesn't have a plausible Christian answer. In our illustration above, imagine if Smith had run from the problem or just tried to ignore the tension. Smith now has the benefit of seeing a solution to this problem.

Asking "What's the problem?" is so important because it forces us to look squarely at an alleged problem and size it up. When we do so we may find a genuine problem, but we may not. It might turn out to be a lot of fuss about nothing. Daring to size up the problem is sometimes all it takes.

The following are some things that may not be as big of a problem as they first appear.

1. Being unable to fully and exhaustively answer a why question. We often wonder why God did things the way that he did. Well, the reality is we will not often get our why questions answered. Even if I don't have a full answer for these why questions, I don't necessarily have a problem. Having unanswered questions is just a part of life. Consider the disciples, for example. They had Jesus in their midst and yet they often didn't understand *all* of what was happening. Again, I don't have full answers for every question. But so what? This doesn't mean Christianity is false. As I've said, we often need enough of our questions answered, but this is a far cry from needing full and exhaustive answers to our questions.

2. Things in Scripture or theology we don't like. People often point out aspects of Christianity they don't like and list that as a problem. There are many things in Scripture I don't like, especially in my less spiritual moments. Some things may even strike me as downright offensive. But this of course doesn't mean Christianity is false. The Bible has a lot to say about the judgment of sin. There's a sense in which we shouldn't enjoy those passages of Scripture. But so what? What's the problem? Just because we don't like something doesn't mean it's a problem for believing it is true.

3. Something incidental to the truth of Christianity. Christians through the ages have done some terrible things. The church has often been embroiled in scandals of one sort or another. There's no denying this. The church has conquered lands, converted people with the sword, participated in the slave trade, and covered up sexual abuse cases, just to name a few. But at the risk of sounding insensitive, we need to ask, "What's the problem?" These things are terrible and those guilty should be justly condemned, but what follows from this for those of us who are not a party to these things? From the fact that people who identify as Christians have done terrible things, it doesn't follow that Christianity is false. In fact, in some of these cases Christian ethical standards were used to (eventually) oppose these activities (e.g., New World slavery). We are going to fail, at times, to do the right thing. But this fact alone isn't a problem for believing that Christianity is true.

Now sometimes when we ask, "What's the problem?" we realize there *is* a problem. When this happens, we need to ask whether the claims being made are true.

Why Think This Claim Is True?

The second way to evaluate a doubt is to determine whether the objection is reasonable. Here we ask, "Why think this claim is true?" Let's say we've encountered an objection and asked, "What's the problem?" and we see that there is a problem. But it's only a problem if it is true and reasonable to believe. So now we ask if the claims are true.

Let's say we hear a news report of the discovery of an ancient Palestinian ossuary that bears the name "Jesus, son of Joseph." The claim is made that they have discovered the physical (that is, unresurrected) remains of Jesus Christ. Is this a problem if it is true? Yes, it is! If Jesus' bodily remains have been found, then clearly Jesus has not risen from the dead and our faith is worthless (1 Corinthians 15:17).

But now we need evidence that this claim is true because this tune has played before (usually around Easter time and often on public television), and let's just say it has not always been a hit. If the ossuary dates early and looks to be authentic, then it would of course be a genuine problem for the Christian faith. If it turns out there are compelling reasons to think the inscription is a modern forgery, then the problem is of course dissolved. But notice the evidence matters here.

Again, doubts do not win by default. There should be reason to think the claim here is true. But that's not all we need. The evidence for the contrary claim (e.g., that Jesus did not rise from the dead) has to be good enough to outweigh the evidence we have to believe (e.g., that Jesus did rise from the dead). The evidence that this ossuary contains the genuine remains of Jesus Christ would have to be strong enough to overcome the rest of the evidence that I have. This is of course possible. If the ossuary dated very early, the inscription was authentic and uniquely picked out Jesus, the remains were a Jewish male's who was crucified with no broken bones, then this would be a grave challenge indeed. But if the evidence is shaky, then we are justified in maintaining belief based on the rest of the evidence we have.

Or, to take another example, suppose someone claims that the story about Jesus is a forgery of pagan myths. The claim is that at the time of Jesus, the idea of a dying and rising god was quite common, and therefore the followers of Jesus must have copied this theme into the story of Jesus to memorialize him. The account of Jesus' resurrection would be no different from any other ancient myth.

The pagan myth claim has been made by some with large national audiences, such as Bill Maher and Stephen Fry. And it gets repeated regularly as if it is a known fact. This would be a significant problem. But only if it's true!

When we ask whether it is true, we see that it is, at best, an extreme stretch of the details. There is no pagan myth story that comes anywhere close to being the same as Jesus and his resurrection. For example, Osiris, who in his death is dismembered, is put back together and comes back to "life" but only to rule the underworld. Osiris is often cited as a clear example of a resurrection story. The only problem is Osiris is not even really resurrected—at least in any similar sense to Jesus—in that his existence is in the land of the dead. Jesus is alive while Osiris remains dead![2]

The accounts in the Gospels also do not have the same literary structure as a typical pagan myth. The Gospels describe Jesus and the events of his life in real and historical terms. C. S. Lewis once remarked about the Gospel of John: "I have been reading poems, romances, vision-literature, legends, myths all my life. I know what they are like. I know that not one of them is like this."[3] If this is to be a myth, then the authors shouldn't have bothered with all the historical details.

Finally, there's no evidence of any borrowing. We can string together broad and general similarities of almost any story with other stories. Let's be honest: if we've watched one rom-com, we've watched them all! And how many stories have a humble hero who goes through terrific struggle but is victorious in the end? There will be at least a dozen movies with this theme this year alone. So we can find similarities for just about anything, but we would need something more substantial to think they are borrowed. Thus, it's just not reasonable to think the followers of Jesus borrowed pagan myths to memorialize him. This claim certainly does not outweigh the historical evidence we have.

The point is that doubts such as these only become effective when they are well justified and overcome the rest of what we know. The overall balance of evidence matters. Doubts and unanswered questions make a difference to the balance, to be sure.

They may count against the overall status of the belief. But they only defeat a belief if there is a genuine problem, the claims are true, and this problem overcomes the rest of our evidence.

Though this is certainly oversimplifying a bit, we should think of the situation as a big set of scales. We must weigh the evidence for and against. When we've taken some time to get some emotional distance, we have to take an honest look at where the evidence leads. We ask what is the cumulative force of the evidence. For a person to have reason to walk away from their faith, the doubts must tip the scales to the falsity of Christianity.

Once again, as we doubt our doubts we are not going to get everything solved. There are going to be things that we don't (yet) know how to solve, and some things we may never get solved. But since we are not aiming at certainty, it doesn't defeat all the rest of our evidence.

Walking Away or Wagering on Christianity?

Does this mean we should walk away from the faith if our evidence outweighs the evidence we have for the truth of Christianity? Well, let's be honest here. I think we need to be open to that possibility. That is, we need to have intellectual integrity and follow the evidence where it leads. But again, having a few questions that bother us is a long way from having an overwhelming amount of evidence against Christianity.

I've been on this journey of leaning into my questions and doubts for more than two decades. Some challenges remain, to be sure. Many of us will be like Sheldon Vanauken, who saw gaps on both sides of the issue (see chap. 3). He found the case for Christianity made it probable but not proven. But it was the gaps in disbelieving that he couldn't countenance.

Blaise Pascal once made the case that when the evidence is to some degree balanced, the wise person ought to wager on the truth of Christianity. Now many people have misunderstood or misapplied Pascal's famous wager. It is sometimes mistakenly thought that Pascal was anti-reason. But Pascal doesn't see faith as contrary to reason. He says, "Men despise religion; they hate it and fear it is true. To remedy this, we must begin by showing that religion is not contrary to reason."[4]

The wager is also not intended to be a standalone argument for God or the truth of Christianity. Pascal is not saying we ought to simply wager on Christianity given a world of other religious and nonreligious options. What he imagines is a situation in which a person's evidence doesn't fully determine whether it is more rational to believe that Christianity is true or not. It's a case in which reason cannot decide.

Pascal says, "According to reason, you can do neither the one thing nor the other; according to reason, you can defend neither of the propositions."[5] But it is not a situation in which we can be neutral. "Yes; but you must wager. It is not optional. You are embarked."[6] We either place our faith in the reality of Christianity or we don't. The idea is that we are living our life—we are embarked—and so we either live our life placing faith in Christ or we don't.

Insofar as it is up to us, Pascal says the wise person ought to wager or bet on the truth of Christianity. Why? He says, "Let us weigh the gain and the loss in wagering that God is. Let us estimate these two chances. If you gain, you gain all; if you lose, you lose nothing. Wager, then, without hesitation that He is."[7] Peter Kreeft explains, "It is like a leap out of a burning building into a cloud of smoke on the street below, out of which has come a voice saying: 'Jump! I'm holding a safety net. I see you even though you can't see me. Trust me. Jump!'"[8] The evidence is split between jumping or not jumping. What the jumping option has going for is the possibility of being saved, but it does carry the risk of not making it. There's no possibility of survival if you don't jump. You ought to jump because the possible payoff is well worth it.

Again, this is not intended to convince the committed unbeliever. The point is simply to say that if the evidence comes in at a tie, then wise people don't abandon their faith. Instead, we ought to lean toward faith until it becomes untenable. This gives us considerable space to investigate and doubt our doubts.

Asking Big Questions

The unexamined life is not worth living.

<small>Socrates</small>

Constant and frequent questioning is the first key to wisdom. . . .
For through doubting we are led to inquiry,
and by inquiry we perceive the truth.

<small>Peter Abelard</small>

As the philosopher Socrates faces the death penalty for trumped-up charges in an unjust trial, he is offered the opportunity to propose an alternative punishment. At first, he suggests getting free meals in the Prytaneum as his consequence but is urged by friends to consider proposing a sentence of a life of silence in exile. The idea is that he would no longer engage in his famous method of questioning others in pursuit of the truth. But Socrates refuses this. Why? Because, as he famously says, "The unexamined life is not worth living."[1] Unable to accept the unexamined life, he accepts instead his sentence of death and drinks his hemlock cocktail, pitying the city for its corruption.

Socrates was well-known for asking questions. And he greatly annoyed the aristocracy of Athens by his questions to such an extent that it cost him his life. But this is because they were cowards and lacked virtue, preferring to have Socrates executed rather than confront the deep questions. Socrates, by contrast, asked questions not just to annoy but to arrive at truth and knowledge.

Doubting our faith can be a difficult experience, but it has value because, if handled well, it forces us to ask the deep and difficult questions we may not otherwise ask. We like comfort. And there's comfort when it all makes sense. When suddenly it doesn't, we are, in a way, forced to get it figured out. We are forced to ask questions and investigate.

We of course do not need to experience doubts and struggles to ask questions. In fact, in this chapter I suggest that questioning and curiosity are part of a proper approach to a deeper faith. It is a way of life that as Christians we should adopt. But we do need to exercise caution. Again, when we wander it's all too easy to get lost. A crucial part of wandering toward God is learning to ask the big questions well.

Seeking Truth

This may be a bit counterintuitive, but to find God I suggest that we not aim most fundamentally at finding God. Wait, what? Aren't we wandering toward God here? We are, but most fundamentally our intellectual wandering ought to be aimed at finding truth. We don't want to merely confirm what we already believe. And I'm convinced that if we aim at truth with an honest heart, we'll find God. The point is that we shouldn't be so committed to the answers that we aren't honest about the questions. We far too often ask questions already knowing the answer to those questions. But if we are to be well-grounded in our pursuit of God, we need to ask these questions with deep honesty.

This might sound controversial, but it really shouldn't. It's adopting the posture of a truth seeker. Once again, it's making the fundamental reason why you believe in God *because* it is true. I think that God is real and Christianity is true, and so at the end of the day I believe these pursuits come together. But if God doesn't exist or if Christianity is false, then I don't want to believe it. I don't want to believe in vain (1 Corinthians 15:14, 17). Too many Christians believe for reasons other than the truth. And then one day they find themselves doubting their faith and realize, as I did, they don't have good reasons to believe. This often amounts to a crisis. And it's not easy to pursue these things amid a crisis.

The same thing holds for alternative worldviews as well. As Christians, we wouldn't want someone merely having blind faith in these views. Wouldn't we want people to question their religious commitments? Well, if so, we need to do the same thing. We need to ask the deep and difficult questions about Christianity. This is how we surface good evidence.

But how do we do this well? Let's first talk about what not to do. There are two extremes we should avoid. As we'll see, neither of these extremes aims at truth.

The Vice of Fundamentalism

The first extreme we should avoid is fundamentalism. Now different people will react very differently to this term *fundamentalism*. For some, it means being an angry and hateful religious zealot. For others, it simply means that a person believes traditional Christian doctrine. What I mean here by being a fundamentalist is to dogmatically believe that Christianity is true without engaging in the proper inquiry of its truth. This is to live an unexamined faith. We simply believe without ever asking why.

The obvious problem with being a fundamentalist is that our beliefs are held accidentally. They are a matter of where we grew up or a matter of social acceptance. Had we been born to Muslim or Buddhist parents, then we would be Muslim or Buddhist. There is nothing wrong with holding to the worldview of our youth so long as we have investigated its truth. But without that investigation we will simply embrace the view as an accident of our birth.

If we want to believe our Christian beliefs for good reasons, then we have to examine the evidence. If we approach it as fundamentalists who blindly believe, then this wouldn't be to aim at truth. It would be to hold our views irrationally (even if those views turn out to be true incidentally).

The Vice of Skepticism

The other extreme to avoid is skepticism. *Skepticism* is another word that is used variously. I use it here in the sense that one is never satisfied by answers. Often it's a refusal to believe anything religious no matter what reasons are given. Unlike the fundamentalist, the skeptic questions everything but never accepts the answers. Often, skepticism, as I think about it, is similar to unbelief. It's a refusal to believe no matter what evidence is given.

Let me illustrate. It's not uncommon for kids to do everything within their power to resist having to go to sleep. When my daughter was little, we would tell her that it was time for bed. She would respond with "Why?" And I would answer that it's important to get our rest. And then she would respond with "Why?" And, if my patience held out, I would say something such as it's important to get our rest for our health, and it makes tomorrow more fun since we won't be too tired. I may have thought this was a pretty good answer. What stronger case could there be for going to bed? But, sure enough, she'd ask why once again.

What's going on here? She's questioning, but is she seeking an answer? No! She's not after the truth. The reality is that she just doesn't want to go to bed. She's resisting my (what I think are) thoughtful answers to her questions. No amount of answers is going to satisfy her because she is not aiming at the truth but stalling bedtime. No matter what I say, she can always stall once more with a *why*.

Unfortunately some seem to approach issues of faith in a similar way. Skeptics are asking questions, to be sure, and even style themselves as inquiring deeply, but they are often not seeking the truth. The skeptic demands evidence, and when evidence is presented, the skeptic says, "I just wish you'd present even a shred of evidence." Evidence is presented, but it doesn't fit the skeptic's narrow paradigm. This kind of religious skeptic doesn't want the answers, and it seems no amount of evidence is going to satisfy them. They walk into the inquiry with their minds made up that they won't believe in God, no matter the evidence.

Even though typically pitted against one another, this ironically puts the religious skeptic and the fundamentalist in the same category. Neither genuinely seeks truth. Fundamentalists plug their ears, resisting any questioning of the faith. Skeptics may ask questions but refuse to accept the evidence and answers that come.

What stands between these extremes is the thoughtful inquirer. The thoughtful inquirer is not given to the vices of fundamentalism or skepticism, as I've defined these. The thoughtful inquirer embodies certain intellectual virtues. Intellectual virtue is a habit or practice that leads to rationality and ultimately truth. Let's look at a few intellectual virtues that are important for asking the big questions well.

The Virtue of Curiosity

Being curious is the practice of asking questions in the search for truth. Curiosity often gets a bad rap and can sometimes get us into trouble (after all, somehow it killed the cat!). But as will be clear, we can overdo any virtue, and doing so will often be detrimental. We can overdo curiosity, and this will cause lots of problems. But curiosity in the appropriate amount and in the appropriate way is a virtue that leads us to truth.

If we don't have a few questions about our faith, how to understand the Bible, and how we should live as Christ-followers, then something, I'd suggest, is amiss. The Christian gospel, in my view, is clear and able to be understood even by children. And the basics of Christianity are not out of anyone's reach. But understanding many parts of the Bible and Christian doctrine is anything but simple and easy. There are as many different interpretations of certain passages as there are commentators. And then there's the questions about whether these claims are true. It's neither easy to say why they are true nor why they are not true. In fact, these matters have exercised the brightest minds who have ever lived. No matter what we believe, we should have some big questions. We should be curious!

Now it might be objected that we are called to a childlike faith rather than a curious faith. It is important to note that the term *childlike faith* is nowhere in Scripture. Jesus does use the example of children (for example, Matthew 18:2-3), but he doesn't use the example of children to make a point about faith. The Bible never calls us to childlike faith, especially understood as a *childish* faith. In fact, the writer of Hebrews challenges us to leave the childish thinking about God (the milk) and to have a mature faith (Hebrews 5:12–6:2).

But children are a great example. While children are often very trusting, they are also *very* curious. And many children beautifully strike the balance between trust and an insatiable curiosity. They ask questions, questions, and more questions. One of my children is especially given to curiosity. She asks questions about *everything*! I sometimes have to cut her off, saying, "Okay sweetie, last question" because if I don't, I won't make it to work on time. However, in all of these questions, I have never once felt that she didn't trust me. She was coming to me with questions precisely because she does trust me. When children ask questions, their attitude is rarely skeptical or cynical (that comes in the teen years!). They are not typically trying to usurp or unseat the authority of their parents. They are simply and intensely curious. They ask awesome questions because they are filled with wonder and awe at what they see.

Another good example of curiosity is those who are newly in love. In a fresh, new love, we want to know everything there is to know about our significant other. We want to know how they think and are intrigued by (what may seem to outsiders to be) minor details of response. Again, we are not questioning them because we don't trust them. We probably trust them to a fault. We are simply curious about the feelings of fresh, new love.

But the feelings of new love don't last forever. We may not be intrigued by our spouses in quite the same way that we were when we first fell in love. But we should still be curious about the other. In a healthy marriage, that feeling of new love should only grow deeper and more mature. If a couple has lost all curiosity for the other, then this is a marriage in trouble. The same goes for faith that lacks all curiosity about matters of faith.

At one point in the ministry of Jesus, he is being intellectually challenged by the elite Jewish religious leaders of the day, to "trap him" (Matthew 22:15). They challenge him in a variety of ways, and in each case Jesus refutes the challenge. In one challenge an expert in the law asks him, "Teacher, which is the greatest commandment in the law?" (v. 36). Now this might not sound like much of a challenge, but Jesus is being asked, out of all the many Old Testament laws, to name the single greatest command. It's a trap because if Jesus singled out one command, then he can be accused of neglecting something else. Jesus effortlessly responds, "Love the Lord your God with all your heart and with all your soul and with all your mind" (v. 37). This, Jesus says, is the greatest and most important of all the commands. This is a well-known verse, but we often miss the fact that Jesus is saying that we are to love God with our *mind*.

What is it to love God with all our mind? At least in part, just like those who are in love, we intellectually seek after God with intense curiosity. We shouldn't approach him blindly and irrationally, as the fundamentalist. And we shouldn't approach skeptically, challenging God and refusing to believe. We approach with intellectual curiosity precisely because we love him and long to know him deeply. We ask questions to know and love him more deeply.

Having Ears to Hear

We also ought to ask our questions with an open mind. Would it surprise you to know that Jesus often taught people to have an open mind? One might be tempted to think of Jesus as rather narrow-minded, and many Christians have earned this perception along the way. We often get locked into a view that is familiar to us. Jesus urged people to have ears to hear and eyes to see (see Matthew 13:11-17). He, of course, was not commenting on their actual ears or eyes, since he was talking to those whose faculties were in good working order. It's that they were too locked into their preconceived ideas to see and hear that the Messiah was there among them.

To ask questions well, we need to be open-minded to a variety of possible answers. Even if something appears bizarre at first glance, it deserves a hearing. We must learn to listen to objections to our views. If it is so obviously false, then we should be able to say why it is false. And when we can show that some objection is false, then we are even more rational in our view. This will often be far more instructive than simply dismissing a view out of hand.

But, like curiosity, we can overdo open-mindedness. G. K. Chesterton once said, "An open mind is a mark of foolishness, like an open mouth. Mouths and minds were made to shut; they were made to open only in order to shut."[2] Chesterton's point, I take it, is not that all open-mindedness is foolishness. It is being overly open-minded to such an extent that we never settle on truth. It's a mark of foolishness to be open to every idea equally all the time. Some ideas are bad ideas, and we don't need to remain as open to them as more plausible claims. But this all turns on the evidence. As evidence comes, our minds should begin to close in on the most rational view. However, we should only settle on the truth with an eye toward new and better evidence. New evidence should always get a hearing. Since not all views are equally reasonable, especially after rational inquiry, if a view proves to be false or irrational, then it is a good and rational idea to count that view out—unless there is newfound evidence that suggests a need for a second look.

Intellectual Steadfastness

When we ask questions, we should do it with an open mind, open to good evidence. We don't want to be so locked into our views that we don't have ears to hear and eyes to see the truth. We want to be open to new evidence, but we don't want to be so open that we get easily persuaded into a new view. With open-mindedness we are open to new evidence, but with steadfastness we stick with our view while we consider the new evidence.

Once we find truth, it is an intellectual virtue to hang on to it even in the face of challenges, which is sometimes called the intellectual virtue of steadfastness. The idea is that we should seek truth in asking questions. We should be intellectually curious about the world and have an open mind to the ideas that come our way. Some of these will challenge what we believe. But we shouldn't just give in to the challenge until we can complete our inquiry. This is especially true when there is social pressure to conform. Unlike the skeptic who doesn't take anything as truth, the steadfast person holds on to what they take to be true, even if it is unpopular, until it proves irrational.

Steadfastness often takes significant courage, especially when there is pressure to believe differently in your social circles. People may get really upset that you are unwilling to conform your beliefs, and may call you names. But social pressure and name-calling isn't a good reason to change your beliefs. It's important to remain steadfast until you are given good reasons for changing your mind. I don't want someone to come to Christian belief just because they are pressured to believe. If one believes because of social pressure, then there's a good chance one will, at some point, disbelieve when social pressures of a different sort come along. I want someone to, with an open mind, consider the evidence for Christianity and believe on the basis of compelling evidence. One should then remain steadfast unless new and outweighing evidence comes along.

My mind has closed on Christianity. I have investigated with an open mind and have found Christianity to be eminently reasonable. And I am open to new evidence. If I come across an objection to Christianity, I am quite willing to give it a hearing. I want to hear what the claim is and what reasons there are to think that it is true. However, I am not going to suspend my Christian beliefs but will hang on to them in the face of challenge. All of the many reasons I have aren't erased just because I have a new challenge. And I will steadfastly and confidently believe my beliefs until they are shown to be false by compelling evidence.

Ask Questions in Community

This process of questioning should never happen in complete isolation. When we go at it alone, we can sometimes get way inside our heads and fail to think carefully and clearly about the ideas and their implications. Instead we should doubt and ask big questions in community. We need people who will walk alongside us, challenging us and pulling us back down to earth as we work through our doubts and questions. In short, we need dialogue partners. We all need a community of like-minded folks in which we can together explore the implications of our view and think about it rationally.

There are a few reasons for this. First, no single person can be familiar with all relevant areas and issues to sufficiently address intellectual questions. It can be so helpful and even feel like a lifeline to have someone who has already seen their way clear on an issue we are struggling with. So if you are struggling, phone a friend! When there are other people involved, we'll necessarily have a broader perspective on that issue. This is true even if we don't completely agree with the perspective offered. As a professor I have the great privilege to present and walk through ideas with students regularly. I'm continually amazed at how my students will often bring a perspective I haven't thought about previously even with ideas I have taught hundreds of times.

Second, wrestling with ideas in community is helpful because expressing ideas to someone else forces us to think through those ideas more carefully. Again, sometimes we can be too much in our heads, unable to make connections and figure out solutions that are staring us in the face. Sometimes ideas seem so incredibly clear to us when we are reflecting on them. Simply expressing it to someone else forces us to lay it all out carefully. It's not uncommon for something that seemed so clear in our minds to be shown to be unclear when we try to express it to someone. It's one thing to feel intellectual tension in our heads when we encounter an objection and it's another thing to have to articulate just what the problem is to someone else.

Third, being in dialogue with people is helpful because others can often see in a way we cannot where we are making unjustified assumptions. Again, it can be very difficult on our own to see our weak points. But when we have someone there to push us on our beliefs, we are going to be more careful and gain new insights into how to work out our intellectual questions.

I think we need like-minded people in this pursuit. That is, we need a Christian community of those who are walking the same or similar journey and who are committed to thinking carefully and rationally about faith. Christians need other Christians who are also wandering toward God. Ideally, we can find someone who is a bit further down the road than we are. But even if it is someone who is asking the same deep and difficult questions about faith, it is wonderful to have a fellow traveler on the journey. Not everyone is going to have the same questions or the same struggles. It's an invaluable benefit to have people there for support, help, and feedback as we lean into our doubts and big questions.

But we also need those who disagree. We need people who will challenge our conclusions because they really do disagree. In my experience this happens best with those who are genuine friends. In other words, although having discussions with those who are hostile and even adversarial can from time to time be helpful, these discussions are always of limited value. The reason for this is that it is easy for our aim to become winning the contest rather than landing on truth and good evidence. Many Christian-atheist debates reduce to mere spitting matches of who can best the other with wit and well-placed zingers. These are often not dialogues aimed at knowing the truth. It is a great blessing to have people in our lives who do care about us but take a very different view on matters and will engage us with thoughtful dialogue.

Reading

As important as community is, it can be difficult to find. How I wish that a typical church congregation would provide the opportunity for people to genuinely ask deep and difficult questions and have room to doubt their faith. But the reality is that this can be quite scarce. Too many Christians are committed to a thin and fundamentalist view of faith. But we all have many, many people with whom we can and should walk in our journey of faith. We may not ever get the opportunity to have a face-to-face conversation, but there are so many who

have given us the gift of their writings. We should avail ourselves of the many books that focus on asking deep and difficult
questions. With books we have the great privilege of having
community with deeply thoughtful people who will challenge
us to think carefully on our journey toward God.

There are many terrific recent books, but we also cannot
neglect being acquainted with the Christians of old. Now, I
don't naturally gravitate to reading old books, but I know that
I neglect these at my peril. I've had to force myself to become
friends with these ancient saints and sages and allow them to
speak wisdom, and the wisdom they speak is incredible. So
though this can be a battle, you need to know the extraordinary
value there is in reading old books. C. S. Lewis once said,

> Every age has its own outlook. It is specially good at
> seeing certain truths and specially liable to make certain
> mistakes. We all, therefore, need the books that will
> correct the characteristic mistakes of our own period.
> And that means the old books. All contemporary writers
> share to some extent the contemporary outlook—even
> those, like myself, who seem most opposed to it. . . . None
> of us can fully escape this blindness, but we shall certainly
> increase it, and weaken our guard against it, if we read
> only modern books. Where they are true they will give us
> truths which we half knew already. Where they are false
> they will aggravate the error with which we are already
> dangerously ill. The only palliative is to keep the clean sea
> breeze of the centuries blowing through our minds, and
> this can be done only by reading old books.[3]

The point here is old books come at things with a different set of assumptions and force us to question ours. Whereas contemporary books, even books arguing for an opposing worldview, probably share many of the same and perhaps faulty assumptions.

But here's the thing. Many Christians read only popular-level books if they read at all. As a Christian you stand in a long and rich intellectual tradition, and to neglect the old books is to neglect a rich repository of truth and wisdom. It is often the case that the most difficult objections to Christianity were already raised by Christians who grappled deeply with their faith. You should check out the gold in Augustine, Anselm, Aquinas, Dante Alighieri, Duns Scotus, the Reformers, Blaise Pascal, Jonathan Edwards, G. K. Chesterton, C. S. Lewis, and many more. Often these ancient thinkers provided a robust answer to the deep and difficult objections many centuries ago. Find help in community if you can, but your books will be your friends and your guides.

Don't be afraid to ask your questions. Be curious! Have an open mind and then be steadfast in the truth as you find it. Take this one step at a time. You will begin to make your way and grow in your understanding and knowledge. It can be hard work but well worth the journey.

The Reason for God

The sum total of all possible knowledge of God is not possible
for a human being, not even through a true revelation.
But it is one of the worthiest inquiries to see how far
our reason can go in the knowledge of God.

IMMANUEL KANT

It is true, that a little philosophy inclineth man's mind to atheism;
but depth in philosophy bringeth men's minds about to religion.

FRANCIS BACON

The heavens declare the glory of God;
and the skies proclaim the work of his hands.

KING DAVID

We've looked at how to think of faith and doubt, as well as
how to ask big questions to grow in our faith. We turn
now to asking some big questions with the aim of providing
reasons to believe. The goal is not to give an exhaustive case for
Christianity. The goal will be to look at a variety of facts that
point us to the truth of Christianity. I will call these "curious
facts." These are facts of our world that most people believe.

But they cry out for an explanation. I argue that the Christian worldview makes good sense of these curious facts.

None of them is a singular slam dunk, and by no means do they *prove* Christianity is true. That is, these will fall short of giving us absolute certainty. Again, the goal is simply to provide reasons to believe. Some will likely be more compelling than others, but it is the cumulative force of these curious facts that constitutes a strong case to believe that Christianity is true. This is a case that can provide confidence to believe in the Christian way as we journey toward God.

Why Think God Exists?

There are perhaps no bigger questions to ask than questions about God. One of the most important worldview issues is to decide whether God exists. Even if we come to think that God does not exist, this has a big impact on how we think about the world. But of course if there is a God, this too is a game-changer.

It's important to mention that the notion of God I have in mind is unapologetically loaded. By "God" I don't mean just any notion of God. I mean a being who is personal and transcendent, who created the universe, who is perfect in all ways, and who is sovereign over all. By *personal*, I mean that God has a mind with conscious thoughts and a will. By *transcendent*, I mean that God is not within the physical, material world but exists outside of it. This is a being who has every perfection (that is, all-powerful, perfectly good, all-knowing, and so on) and is the ultimate and necessary source of all reality. I am not interested in gods, such as the Greek and Roman gods, who are neither transcendent nor perfect. I don't have in mind a god as an impersonal force. These are not beings worthy of our worship. It's only the perfect God who stands outside the universe having created it and us, is sovereign over all, and to whom we owe worship. And when it comes to the slate of curious facts, they point to the existence of this sort of God. In short, it is only this notion of God that explains the world as we find it.

There are many reasons Christians have proposed to believe that God exists. In 1986, prominent Christian philosopher Alvin Plantinga famously suggested there were "two dozen (or so)" good arguments for God's existence.[1] Many new and novel arguments for God's existence have been developed since Plantinga suggested this over thirty-five years ago. The point is that there are *a lot* of arguments for God, and whole books have been written to develop the various arguments. Some of these get very technical and are of limited value for those without advanced degrees in philosophy, science, and related areas. However, I'm convinced that everyone encounters reasons in everyday life that point to the reality of God.

Why doesn't everyone believe in God? Why are there atheists? Well, it's possible to resist all this evidence, and many people do. We can ignore the evidence for God, we can be distracted from it, and we can even convince ourselves that God does not exist. As C. Stephen Evans has put it, the evidence for God is *widely available* but, at the same time, *easily resistible.*[2]

The apostle Paul says it this way:

What may be known about God is plain to them, because God has made it plain to them. For since the creation of the world God's invisible qualities—his eternal power and divine nature—have been clearly seen, being understood from what has been made, so that people are without excuse. (Romans 1:19-20)

God can be clearly seen in the world, but Paul goes on to describe the ways humanity has resisted and denied his existence. He says, "They exchanged the truth about God for a lie, and worshiped and served created things rather than the Creator" (v. 25). But don't miss his point. The world is replete with God's handiwork, and with eyes to see, we can encounter this compelling evidence.

The World as the Handiwork of God

We begin with the variety of ways in which the world looks to be the handiwork of God.

Curious fact 1: The universe exists. I realize this may strike you as an unimpressive start. But think for a moment how curious it is that the universe exists. It's an amazing thing. There seems to be no reason to think it must exist. It didn't have to exist, but it does. What's more, many cosmologists think that the universe began to exist at a finite time ago. This beginning is often referred to as the *big bang.* But how could the universe simply bang into existence from no cause? Perhaps there is a universe-generating mechanism out there that is completely impersonal and natural. It just spits out universes. Now there is no evidence for this sort of mechanism, so it's not an idea to take too seriously. But what's important to see is that it too would be contingent. It didn't have to exist, so it makes sense to ask why it exists. What we need is something that explains these things that isn't itself contingent.

These thoughts have led some of the brightest minds through history to think that to explain the contingency of the universe, it must have a transcendent and necessary cause that has brought it about. God fits the job description here.

Now we should notice that I didn't formalize this argument and stayed away from most of the technical details. While I'm happy to have that kind of a discussion, it's all too easy to get bogged down in the technicality. This is an obvious (and yet curious) fact of reality. I'm also not claiming that, on the basis of this claim, one must therefore believe that God exists. I am simply saying that a transcendent, personal God, who is the ultimate and necessary source of all, well explains the existence of the universe. This provides *a* reason to believe. More evidence may show that a different explanation is called for. But, by my lights, God's existence is a compelling explanation of the universe itself.

But it's not just the fact that the universe exists that seems to point to God. It's the kind of universe it is. It is quite curious that there are conscious beings who exist on a planet with a suitable environment along with the rest of biological life.

Curious fact 2: The world exhibits exquisite design. The universe curiously seems designed with us in mind. Even if a universe popped into existence from a purely natural source, it is very unlikely that there would be beings like you and me able to reflect on how crazy and wonderful this is. Our ability to think, move our bodies, create, craft, invent, do science, advance in technology, and generally thrive in a world that hangs together in unbelievably intricate ways raises a certain question: Why?

The more we learn about the nature of our universe, the more we see how improbable it is that it would have simply developed this way. The parameters for a life-permitting universe have turned out to be very narrow indeed. These parameters include conditions and certain numerical constants that had to be built into the universe from the very beginning. These include such things as the low entropy state of the early universe, the strong and weak nuclear forces, and the gravitational force. It is not just that these need to each be dialed in exactly as they are, but they must be balanced together in very specific ways for this to be a life-permitting universe.[3]

Beyond these cosmic conditions are so-called local conditions that make our planet habitable. And there are a great number of these conditions. For example, planet Earth is, in a way, protected by Jupiter and Saturn. These massive planets absorb objects into their gravitational force that would otherwise cause mass extinction were they to hit Earth. Also, our unique moon is necessary for life. The large size of our moon causes our planet to actually tilt on its axis, which helps keep the climate of our planet relatively constant. Water is of course important for life and it has several unique properties. Water is oddly less dense in its solid state (that is, when it freezes). If it wasn't, ice would sink and bodies of water would freeze from the bottom up, which would kill off the aquatic life, causing massively harmful effects to the Earth's ecosystem. Instead, water freezes from the top-down, allowing aquatic life to thrive. Lastly, the size of Earth is necessary for the strength of our magnetic field as this holds our atmosphere in place. If it were different, our atmosphere would become unstable or dissipate into outer space.[4]

Now unless you are a science major, some of this might be a bit over your head. And that's okay. The point is these are well-established facts about the universe that make life on earth unbelievably improbable without a designer. It's curious that the world has what seems to be exquisite design.

Suppose that you and I are astronauts and are on a mission to Mars. Suppose things go badly and we are stranded on the surface of Mars. We have our space suits, but they are running out of oxygen quickly. Things look quite bleak until we come upon a structure. We enter the structure, and to our great surprise we find a fully functional biosphere constructed in such a way that there's everything we need for survival and much more as well. We can take off our space suits because there's oxygen and the biosphere's temperature is a balmy 72 degrees. There are massive stocks of food—and good food as well. There's exercise equipment and a library full of interesting books. Oh, and there's even a home theater with subscriptions to all of the streaming services!

What would we think? We would know that someone had designed this biosphere with us (or at least people like us) in mind. The world may not come to us ready-made with Netflix, but when we consider what must be the case for a life-permitting universe, it looks like the handiwork of God. Theoretical physicist Paul Davies says,

> Scientists are slowly waking up to an inconvenient truth—
> the universe looks suspiciously like a fix. The issue

concerns the very laws of nature themselves. For 40 years, physicists and cosmologists have been quietly collecting examples of all too convenient "coincidences" and special features in the underlying laws of the universe that seem to be necessary in order for life, and hence conscious beings, to exist. Change any one of them and the consequences would be lethal. Fred Hoyle, the distinguished cosmologist, once said it was as if "a super-intellect has monkeyed with physics."[5]

Now, Davies doesn't think this means God exists. Davies hopes that we can explain this apparent design from looking within the universe. But the point seems like it can hardly be denied that the apparent design just might be actual design. That is, God's existence provides a satisfying explanation of these life-permitting features of the universe.

And we don't have to go to astrophysics and cosmology to see the exquisite design. Typical life experience is itself extraordinary and entirely curious. Even mundane actions involve an incredible number of functions and processes as we move through the world without a problem. Sometimes we become most cognizant of the exquisite design of our bodies when something has gone wrong. Our bodies, from the functioning of our major systems down to the information contained in our DNA, are exquisitely curious.

We also live in a day and age of amazing technological advances. How is it that we can construct skyscrapers, carry supercomputers in our pockets, and put humans on the moon? We may not know how it all works, but we know that it indeed does work, and we all benefit from it. Technological advances can only happen in a world that can be understood and manipulated. But this, too, is curious. Albert Einstein once said, "One may say 'The eternal mystery of the world is its comprehensibility.' . . . The fact that it is comprehensible is a miracle." Einstein goes on to talk about the extraordinary connection of our concepts with "the complexes of sense experiences."[6] The point is the world is wondrously amazing and we are able to do wondrously amazing things in it and it didn't have to be this way.

What would explain all of this? Again, the point is not that this evidence absolutely proves God's existence. But these extraordinary and curious features are well explained by the existence of a creating and supremely intelligent God.

Right and Wrong as a Divine Clue

We turn from the physical world of what is to the moral world of oughts and obligations. We live in a world seemingly governed by standards. That is, there are ways humans *ought* to behave. For example, what I'm about to say will seem abhorrent. You, if you have any moral sense at all, will think it would be wrong to do this, even if one could get away with it. Here it is: suppose a grown man punches a child in the face as hard as he can because he thinks the child is ugly. This seems morally wrong no matter what. There seems to be no way to put this in a different light no matter the context. In short, it is objectively wrong. It doesn't matter what the culture is or the historical era, and it doesn't matter if one is an atheist or a theist. It's just wrong. Obvious, right? But this obviousness is part of the point and leads us to the following fact.

Curious fact 3: Objective moral standards exist. Almost everyone believes in or at least acts like these standards exist. We may debate the applications of these moral standards, but for many, at least for some standards, they are intuitively obvious. Take, for example, recent movements such as Black Lives Matter, All Lives Matter, Blue Lives Matter, #MeToo, #ChurchToo, the pro-life and pro-choice movements, or thinking the church is an evil institution or an institution of virtue and value. No matter where you fall on these highly charged issues, notice each of these assumes the existence of moral facts. Black ("all" or "blue") lives only matter if they have moral value. The church is evil (or an institution of virtue and value) if only there are such things as moral standards.

But if God doesn't exist, how do we explain why these things are right or wrong? This is a difficult case to make. But notice: if God does exist, then objective morals make good sense.

Let's be clear. We are not asking whether nontheists are moral people. Of course, they often are! Sometimes they do better than their religious counterparts. I am not implying that a nontheist can't believe in moral facts even if they don't believe God exists. Again, almost everyone in the world believes in moral facts and live as if moral facts exist. I am simply asking how we explain those facts.

In the Christian view, God is righteous in all of his ways. In this we have an objective moral standard or ideal. God gives us a variety of commands in the Bible and as Romans 2:15 says, God's laws are written on our hearts. These commands make sense as a reflection of his righteous character. God himself is the moral standard and grounds objective morality.

Human Value and Purpose

Also in the moral dimension there is something very special in this universe. It is that we—all of us—count as special, and because of this what we do in life counts as well. Humans have value not derived from what anyone does. We have value just for being human.

Curious fact 4: Humans have intrinsic value. Almost everyone believes that humans have value. It is not just that we ascribe value when someone is of value to us (for example, our children, family members, or friends), but we think that in general people violate something deep and fundamental when they intentionally kill or even harm another human being. This holds true for people who look very different from us and have different cultural habits from us. This also holds true even if the human lacks rational capacities (such as newborn babies and the mentally handicapped). We seem to think if one is human, then they have value no matter what. But this is a curious fact. How do we explain it?

Could we explain it by saying we've socially evolved toward this end? The problem with the social Darwinist view is that evolutionary explanations only work on the basis of survival advantage. Is there a survival advantage for universally treating people with dignity and respect? History seems to say no, at least not in all circumstances. Societies have thrived with slave classes and with the devaluing of neighboring societies. Think about it. A society tends to do very well when it has free labor. This is of course morally abhorrent, but this abhorrent behavior has economic advantage. Ancient Rome lasted twelve centuries despite the fact that only male Roman citizens had genuine rights and it had a slave class! It's costly to protect the rights of every single human. It's morally praiseworthy but it does not add survival advantage. Thus the social Darwinist view doesn't explain moral facts very well at all.

The evolutionary explanation of morality may explain why we *believe* this. Perhaps there is survival advantage for people to believe there are moral standards. But it wouldn't explain human value itself. Human value and rights would be a matter of social conventions. Human value would not be intrinsic or objective, since we could have evolved to believe quite differently. On this view, we would not have a good explanation of the fact of intrinsic human value itself. And if there's no God, it seems difficult to ground why the species Homo sapiens is any different from any other biological life.

I again want to be quick to make the point that a person can believe that all humans are intrinsically valuable even if they believe there is no God. They can also treat all people as valuable. But the pressing question is, How does one explain this fact? Consider the two statements made by documents crucially important for our contemporary society.

First, the US Declaration of Independence, says, "We hold these truths to be self-evident, that all men are created equal, that they are endowed by their Creator with certain unalienable Rights."[7] Now consider the UN Declaration of Human Rights: "All human beings are born free and equal in dignity and rights. They are endowed with reason and conscience and should act towards one another in a spirit of brotherhood."[8]

Do you notice a significant difference between these two statements? They agree in declaring universal rights, and this is a very good thing. But the UN Declaration leaves blank any explanation for why we are all equal in dignity and rights. The US Declaration includes a *ground* (i.e., an explanation) for thinking all human beings are equal in certain unalienable rights. We have these rights precisely because God has endowed us with them.

A nontheist can perfectly well follow the UN Declaration and treat all human beings with respect and dignity. Full stop. Again, sometimes nontheists do better than Christians in treating each other with dignity. But treating people with equality and dignity is one thing; having a solid ground or explanation for doing so is an entirely different matter.

Again, the fact that we all value others and live as if we have significance is well explained by the existence of God, who, so to speak, endows our lives with significance and value. In the Christian view we are not merely molecules in motion; nor are we simply more advanced slime. We are embodied souls bearing the image of God, designed to glorify God. Our dignity and value, therefore, are not primarily found in our high level of neurological and biological functioning. There is something much deeper within our nature as humans. We can look different and act different from other humans, but this does not change our intrinsic natures. This deep intrinsic notion seems to track perfectly with the way we value human lives.

Bumping into God

The final reason many people believe in God is because, well, they run into him. From time to time people have direct experiences of God himself. This is when we have experiences that are not best explained in any way other than that God exists. I'll call these "religious experiences."

Curious fact 5: People have religious experiences. It is very common for people to report having experiences that seem to be supernatural. These include such things as miraculous events, healings, answers to prayer, and an overwhelming sense of the presence of the divine.

Having a direct experience of something is typically an ideal reason for believing that the thing exists. We may have all the reason in the world to think something does not exist until that thing shows up and says hi. However, direct experience of God is often criticized, not so much because folks don't have amazing stories that are difficult to explain away, but because these reports are quite common and point in too many different directions. Christians have stories, Mormons have stories, Muslims have stories, Hindus have stories, spiritualists have stories, and on and on. Sometimes the threshold of evidence seems very low. Far too many things get labeled as a miracle when probably it is just a surprising coincidence. Was getting that prime parking spot on Easter Sunday morning at church a miracle? Well, probably not.

Still, many people report having experienced the divine. Divine experiences also play a significant role throughout the Bible. And it seems to me that if God exists, we should expect there to be numerous reports of experiences of God, and if these reports are reliable, then this should constitute evidence that God exists.

To be clear, I do agree with critics who say not every report could be accurate. For some reason people make up stories. Other times, people unintentionally make mistakes of interpretation.

Direct experiences can be the most powerful evidence a person has, but at the same time, experiences have at least two liabilities. First, it is easy to misinterpret experiences. We have to be very careful and judicious with what we take an experience to *mean*. What happens is one thing; what it all means is another. So, we should be very hesitant to read too much into what we take to be a religious experience.

Second, experiences of God are often very individualistic. They are not typically repeatable or sharable affairs as experiences. You can tell someone about an experience you've had, but you can't always cause the person to share the same experience as you. This may be powerful evidence for you, but it's testimonial evidence for the rest of us. Testimonial evidence can still of course be evidence, but it's not as powerful compared to direct experience.

With all this said, people have had wild experiences that seem to be experiences of God. This of course makes sense if God exists. While perhaps some of these stories can be explained away, it is surely rational to think that some point to the existence of God.

Conclusion

We have seen in this chapter five curious facts.

- Curious fact 1: The universe exists.
- Curious fact 2: The world exhibits exquisite design.
- Curious fact 3: There exist objective moral standards.

- Curious fact 4: Humans have intrinsic value.
- Curious fact 5: We have religious experiences.

Each of these is well explained by the existence of God. We are a long way from proving the existence of the God of Abraham, Isaac, Jacob, and Jesus. It's true we haven't argued directly for the existence of the Christian God. But what we should notice is that the Christian God is entirely consistent with this evidence. I haven't ruled out all other possible views that are likewise consistent. My aim has been to provide reasons for confidence that a God of this sort exists. We turn in chapter eight to provide reasons for confidence in a specifically Christian view.

Something Extraordinary Happened

I know the resurrection is a fact, and Watergate proved it to me.
How? Because 12 men testified they had seen Jesus raised
from the dead, then they proclaimed that truth for 40 years,
never once denying it. Every one was beaten, tortured, stoned
and put in prison. They would not have endured that if it weren't
true. Watergate embroiled 12 of the most powerful men in
the world—and they couldn't keep a lie for three weeks.
You're telling me 12 apostles could keep a lie for 40 years?
Absolutely impossible.

CHUCK COLSON

Lord, to whom shall we go? You [Jesus] have the words of
eternal life. We have come to believe and to know that
you are the Holy One of God.

SIMON PETER

There are many different narratives out there for how to understand God. Different religious traditions describe God quite differently. So we need some reasons for thinking that Christianity has it right. I will begin by arguing that Jesus, his teaching, and the movement he started are quite unique compared to the alternatives.

Just as before, I'm not intending to prove Christianity but only to provide reasons to believe it's true. Again, I find these compelling and they give me confidence that Christianity is indeed true.

Jesus as a Standout

When I was doubting my faith while in seminary, I was specifically struggling with why I should believe in Christianity over other religious traditions. It struck me that I had largely believed that Christianity was true because I grew up in a Christian tradition. It seemed I would be a Muslim if I grew up in a Muslim tradition or a Buddhist from growing up in a Buddhist tradition. It all seemed very incidental.

As I leaned into the doubts and began to investigate, I quickly realized that Christianity was unlike most religious traditions because it was based on events for which there is historical evidence. Jesus came into history in real time and at a real place, he publicly performed miracles and taught with authority, ultimately showing that he is from God by rising from the dead. It struck me that the Bible itself pins the whole truth of Christianity on the historicity of the resurrection. As we've seen Paul say, "If Christ has not been raised, your faith is futile" (1 Corinthians 15:17).

As I took a look at other religions, I came to realize how extraordinary this fact is for Christianity. It is exceedingly rare for a religious tradition to appeal to evidence at all, much less make the whole thing turn on the historicity of one event.

What's nice is that this focuses our investigation. If the resurrection didn't happen, we don't need to bother with the Bible's many other claims. But if it did happen, then there's reason to believe the rest. So let's ask this big question: Are there reasons to believe that Jesus rose from the dead?

The first reason we'll consider for the historicity of the resurrection is that people made this claim very early. The reason this is important is that if no one made this claim until centuries later, then of course we would chalk this up to being a mere legend. Legends start with people telling stories. Stories, as they are told again and again, can sometimes tend to get bigger and more dramatic. Jesus, by virtually all accounts, had a following of people who passed on stories about him. If there was a large time gap between Jesus' life and the first claim of his resurrection, then the very reasonable inference would be that this is a story that got bigger and bigger. Jesus was just a desert rabbi that turned into the God-man dying and rising from the dead.

But if the accounts date early, then legendary development is rather unlikely. Legends take time to develop. People don't tend to make up elaborate stories immediately. Why? It's because eyewitnesses are still in the picture, and eyewitnesses have a regulating effect. Somebody can't just spin a wild yarn if the people involved are all still present. So if we can get close enough to the event, then it's much more likely to be historical.

Close

Let's zoom out to the turn of the first century (AD 100) and look first at a non-Christian source. Around this time there is a Roman historian by the name of Tacitus writing about the history of Rome from the time of the emperors Tiberius (AD 14) to Nero (AD 54). The ministry of Christ falls squarely within this time, including the time of his death at around AD 33. In discussing Nero, Tacitus writes of Nero falsely accusing Christians of the great fire of Rome and for his ruthless persecution. According to Tacitus,

> Nero substituted as culprits, and punished in the utmost refinements of cruelty, a class of men, loathed for their vices, whom the crowd styled Christians. Christus, the founder of the name, had undergone the death penalty in the reign of Tiberius, by sentence of the procurator Pontius Pilatus, and the pernicious superstition was checked for a moment, only to break out once more, not merely in Judea, the home of the disease, but in the capital itself, where all things horrible or shameful in the world collect and find a vogue.[1]

It's clear that Tacitus is not a fan of Christianity. He calls it a "pernicious superstition" that has broken out throughout Judea and the city of Rome. This implies that it has broken out across a huge swath of area. It is no isolated Jewish cult by the time Nero is in power, which is less than thirty-five years later.

What is this "pernicious superstition" that has made its way to the consciousness of a Roman emperor to the degree that it has earned his ire? Could we plausibly believe that it is Jesus' moral teaching? To me, the teachings "Blessed are the peacemakers, for they will be called children of God" and "If anyone slaps you on the right cheek, turn to them the other cheek also" aren't "vices" worthy of punishments of "the utmost refinements of cruelty." For a Roman emperor to be bothered with this, we need something far more extraordinary.

We know what the New Testament identifies as the extraordinary claim Christians are making at this time: Jesus Christ rose from the dead. That's a claim that would rankle a Roman emperor. Jesus' resurrection implies that Jesus is no mere man and that he deserves to be worshiped and followed *by all*—including Roman emperors! It seems reasonable to think that Christians were claiming, as the New Testament reports, that Jesus was raised from the dead, and this would be within about thirty-five years of Jesus' crucifixion.

This might sound like a long time, and indeed a lot can happen in thirty-five years. But even if this is as close as we could get, there would likely be some eyewitnesses even if many of them now would be rather old. The point is that even with this late date from an extrabiblical source, this already puts the claims of Jesus' resurrection within the lifetime of at least some eyewitnesses.

Closer

But thirty-five years is indeed quite a bit of time, so let's zoom in a bit further. We'll begin with the book of Acts, which reads as a rather factual narrative and purports to provide the history of the early church from its inception. The book of Acts ends rather abruptly. After a buildup of Paul's journeys and eventual arrest, it ends with Paul awaiting trial in Rome. This is strange since we know there were catastrophic events that occurred just after this time. For example, we know that the Jewish temple in Jerusalem is destroyed in a brutal assault by Rome in

AD 70. But the book of Acts is silent on this event. We also know that James the brother of Jesus is martyred during this time as is the apostle Paul (AD mid-60s). Both James and Paul feature in the book of Acts. The book of Acts records the death of other early leaders of the church (for example, Stephen in Acts 7 and James the apostle in Acts 12:1-2). But it is silent on these events. It would have been especially natural for it to conclude with the death of Paul since Paul emerges as the central character in the latter half of the book. What plausibly explains this silence? Many scholars think it ends in this abrupt way because it was finished *before* these events occurred.

This plausibly dates the book of Acts to the early to mid-60s. The author of the book of Acts is Luke, who is also the author of the Gospel of Luke. It is widely believed that the Gospel of Luke was written before the book of Acts. We can take one further step. Many biblical scholars think the Gospel of Mark was written before Luke. We don't know how many years separated these books. So to be judicious with this evidence, it seems plausible to think a complete Gospel was written somewhere between twenty and thirty years after the events it describes.

This still sounds to our modern ears like an extraordinary amount of time. We are used to hearing reports practically in real time about events that may be happening on the other side of the globe! But when it comes to ancient accounts, twenty to thirty years is extraordinarily good. For example, Tacitus is widely considered to be one of the greatest of all ancient historians, and his *Annals* is his crowning achievement. The *Annals* detail history involving the Roman Empire in the first century.

But Tacitus writes the *Annals* in the early second century, some fifty to eighty years after the dates it describes. And yet this is considered a very reliable historical source. Or there's Plutarch's *Life of Alexander*, which is a historical biography of Alexander the Great, that gives historical details about Alexander and his campaigns not found in any other sources. Plutarch lived some four hundred years after Alexander! So twenty to thirty years is quite good by comparison. Twenty to thirty years would certainly be within the lifetimes of many eyewitnesses.

Ridiculously Close

But here's where it gets extraordinary. We can zoom in even further. Many people do not realize that the letters of Paul are the earliest documents of the New Testament, and many of them are regarded by even critical scholars as authentic (especially 1-2 Corinthians, Galatians, and Romans). These are typically dated to the mid-50s, which places them just over twenty years after Jesus' ministry. This would be earlier than the Gospel of Mark. Paul is typically writing to Christians who already believe in and know the details of Jesus' resurrection. So he doesn't typically take the time to describe the historical events surrounding the resurrection. But he does discuss it several times—including in Romans 1:4, 6:5; Philippians 3:10; and 1 Thessalonians 4:14—and it's always of crucial theological importance.

The likely response to this is that we still have a considerable amount of time between the events and the accounts. There's still a solid twenty years between these accounts and the alleged event. It would be nice if we could get closer than this. And indeed we can.

If a twenty-year gap is quite good, what follows simply boggles the mind!

New Testament scholars can discern when a portion of the text is an early creed. A creed is a formulation of key doctrine set in a memorable and summarized fashion. The thing about a creed is that it dates earlier than the text it is embedded in since the creed is already in use. First Corinthians 15 begins with an early Christian creed. Paul says:

> What I received I passed on to you as of first importance: that Christ died for our sins according to the Scriptures, that he was buried, that he was raised on the third day according to the Scriptures, and that he appeared to Cephas, and then to the Twelve. After that, he appeared to more than five hundred of the brothers and sisters at the same time, most of whom are still living, though some have fallen asleep. Then he appeared to James, then to all the apostles, and last of all he appeared to me also, as to one abnormally born. (vv. 3-8)

The big question is, when did Paul receive this creed? Determining this helps determine when to date the creed itself. John Dominic Crossan says,

> Paul wrote to the Corinthians from Ephesus in the early 50s C.E. But he says in 1 Corinthians 15:3 that "I handed on to you as of first importance which I in turn received." The most likely source and time for his reception of that tradition would have been Jerusalem in the early 30s when, according to Galatians 1:18, he "went up to Jerusalem to visit Cephas [Peter] and stayed with him fifteen days."[2]

Did you catch that? This places the dating of this creed, according to Crossan, in the "early 30s," when Paul would have had contact with the other apostles. Jesus died when? In the early 30s! This dates to just after the events it describes, replete with the theological understanding of Jesus' death and resurrection grounded in eyewitness testimony! Not only is this within the lifetimes of the eyewitnesses, Paul names eyewitnesses who are, by all accounts, still very much leaders of the early church.

It is worth pointing out who John Dominic Crossan is. Crossan is one of the cofounders and most prominent members of the Jesus Seminar, a group of liberal scholars who were extremely critical of the biblical accounts of Jesus. Each member of the Jesus Seminar would vote on which sayings of Jesus should be considered authentic. The group only had confidence in about 20 percent of the sayings of Jesus. Crossan is no friend of the gospel, and yet even he thinks this creed dates almost concurrently with the events it recounts.

And this is not unique to Crossan. Critical scholar Gerd Lüdemann grants "that all the elements in the tradition are to be dated to the first two years after the crucifixion of Jesus . . . not later than three years after the death of Jesus."[3] According to New Testament scholar Gary Habermas, "Most of the critical scholars who date these events conclude that Paul received this material within just a few years after Jesus' death, in the early or mid-30s."[4] Habermas goes on to cite dozens of critical scholars who agree.

This is truly exceptional! The account of the most important event in the entire Bible for the Christian tradition dates within a handful of years of the event. The point is that there is simply no time for this to develop as a legend. Legends typically take two or three generations (80–120 years). But the account of Jesus' resurrection arises from the very beginning and is the very same message on which the Christian gospel turns. This is indeed a curious fact.

Curious fact 6: Christians immediately claimed Jesus rose from the dead. Of course, the early Christians could have been lying or mistaken; just because they claim this early on doesn't mean it is necessarily true. But it's an extremely radical claim that seems to come out of nowhere, and this makes the fact that it is claimed from the beginning a curious fact.

The Belief of Jesus' Followers

Imagine this: Jesus is dead. He's been shamefully crucified on a Roman cross. There's no question he's dead. The Romans had made executions a science. It's what they did best. His disciples are dejected and depressed. They are in mourning over the fact that Jesus is dead. It's clear in all four Gospels that none of them expected to see Jesus alive again. Women go to the tomb to anoint Jesus' body with spices (Mark 16:1). The male disciples have secluded themselves for fear of the Jews (John 20:19).

Now, there were other would-be Jewish messiahs around the time of Jesus.[5] In fact, upstart messianic movements were not completely uncommon in those days. However, just like the Jesus movement, they were typically put down by the Roman authorities, the would-be messiahs were executed, and the movements stopped. Occasionally, the movements would restart, but the role of the messiah always transferred to another leader.

What was unthinkable was for the would-be messiah to be executed and the movement to not miss a beat. With his demise, no one would continue thinking of that person as the messiah.

A couple of these messianic movements were referenced by the Pharisee Gamaliel in his speech to the Sanhedrin in Acts 5. Peter and the apostles were imprisoned and ordered to stop preaching about Jesus. The apostles refused, and this enraged the Sanhedrin, who were about to execute all of them, except that Gamaliel offered some wise advice. He referenced two previous failed messianic movements and said,

> Some time ago Theudas appeared, claiming to be somebody, and about four hundred men rallied to him. He was killed, and all his followers were dispersed, and it all came to nothing. After him, Judas the Galilean appeared in the days of the census and led a band of people in revolt. He too was killed, and all his followers were scattered. (Acts 5:36-37)

The wisdom Gamaliel offers is that these clearly were movements of "human origin." Why is this clear? Because the movements were put down. But if the Jesus movement is from God, he says, "You will not be able to stop these men; you will only find yourselves fighting against God" (Acts 5:38-39).

The Jesus movement didn't stop. In an entirely unprecedented move, the followers of Jesus continued to see Jesus as the leader of their movement. Despite his shameful death, they continued to proclaim him as Messiah.

Curious fact 7: Christians proclaimed Jesus as Messiah even though he had been shamefully executed. The reason why this is so curious is because of what the Jewish Messiah was supposed to do. The dominant thought of the day was that the Messiah would free the Jews from Roman rule and oppression and set up a political kingdom ruled by the Jewish Messiah. As the disciples on the road to Emmaus say, "We had hoped that he was the one who was going to redeem Israel" (Luke 24:21). This is why it was so difficult for the Jews to accept Jesus during his ministry: he seemed to have no interest in politics.

Even Jesus' disciples continue to misunderstand this. After Jesus has risen from the dead and he's about to ascend to the Father, his disciples ask, "Lord, are you at this time going to restore the kingdom to Israel?" (Acts 1:6). After all of this they are wondering if Jesus would finally become the political leader they had been expecting all along.

So when Jesus is executed as a common criminal by Rome, it is virtually unthinkable that he is the Messiah. N. T. Wright says,

> Jesus had not done what Messiahs were supposed to do. He had neither won a decisive victory over Israel's political enemies, nor restored the Temple (except in the most ambiguous symbolic fashion). Nor had he brought God's justice and peace to the world; the wolf was not yet lying down with the lamb. But the early gospel traditions are already shaped by the belief that Jesus was Israel's Messiah; Paul regularly calls him *Christos*. . . . For Revelation, Jesus is the Lion of the tribe of Judah. The historian is bound to face the question: once Jesus had been crucified, why would anyone say that he was Israel's Messiah?[6]

Given the execution, everyone should just go home, mourn the loss, and get back to their lives.

Again, this is what they initially do. But not for long. The disciples do an abrupt about-face. They don't stay cooped up in mourning for long. As I've already pointed out, they immediately begin to proclaim Jesus had risen from the dead. The disciples' message is radical: Jesus *is* the Messiah even though he was shamefully executed.

On top of all of this, the disciples face extreme persecution and most die a martyr's death *for* the claims of the gospel. We have no historical record of any of the disciples recanting these claims. Rather, it seems each of them went to death claiming that Jesus rose from the dead.

What Could Change the Disciples' Minds?

It would have to take something extraordinary to change the mind of these disciples about their belief that this messianic movement with Jesus at the helm was over. Many have proposed alternative theories to explain why Jesus' followers claimed he had risen from the dead. These can sometimes be quite elaborate but also often quite unimpressive. Some have proposed that Jesus didn't really die but just appeared dead. But if this is true, why would they worship him as the risen Messiah? They might think he was the luckiest person to survive the expertise involved in a Roman execution, but they would not likely take him to be the risen Christ. Others have proposed that Jesus had an identical twin who rolled into town just after Jesus was crucified, and his followers mistook the twin brother for Jesus. Or it has been proposed that Jesus really was crucified but the disciples had uniform hallucinations that Jesus rose from the dead.

The problem is that none of these are very plausible. What's more they don't seem to be enough to change the minds of the disciples to the point they are willing to sacrifice their very lives.

What would radically change the minds of the disciples that the crucified Jesus is indeed the Messiah to the extent they would give their lives to this view? It seems experiencing Christ raised from the dead would turn the trick! This is the ultimate game-changer for them. Why would they continue to proclaim Jesus is the Messiah? It's because Jesus showed back up risen from the dead. Their Messiah is alive and commissions them to take this gospel message to the ends of the earth. And the disciples forsake their lives and livelihoods and do just that.

Conclusion

There are of course many other reasons we could give for believing that Jesus rose from the dead.[7] My claim here is that there are two curious facts that need explanation:

- Curious fact 6: Christians immediately claimed Jesus rose from the dead.
- Curious fact 7: Christians proclaimed Jesus as Messiah even though he had been shamefully executed.

We need something that explains why the claim shows up so early before there is time for legends to develop and that would radically change the minds of Jesus' disciples. It would have to be so radical that it caused them to immediately proclaim that Jesus rose from the dead and should be thereby worshiped as

Messiah. Though there are of course other proposed explanations, the best and most straightforward explanation is to take them at their word. The disciples experienced the risen Christ, and this propelled the Christian movement throughout the Western Mediterranean to Rome and to the ends of the earth.

Our Deepest Longings

The gospel is not a doctrine of the tongue, but of life. It cannot be grasped by reason and memory only, but it is fully understood when it possesses the whole soul and penetrates to the inner recesses of the heart.

JOHN CALVIN

The music of the Gospel leads us home.

FREDERICK W. FABER

This story begins and ends in joy. It has pre-eminently the 'inner consistency of reality.' There is no tale ever told that men would rather find was true, and none which so many sceptical men have accepted as true on its own merits. For the Art of it has the supremely convincing tone of Primary Art, that is, of Creation. To reject it leads either to sadness or to wrath.

J. R. R. TOLKIEN

Virtually everyone would agree that life can at times be less than satisfying. To be sure, we can sometimes find exhilarating happiness. People do, in fact, win the lottery, both metaphorically and literally, and find themselves on top of the world.

But lottery winners also quickly realize that money doesn't satisfy. Quite a number of them lose all their wealth in short order and find themselves in even more miserable situations than they were in before they got their winnings. The point is that those great moments of life have the annoying tendency to fade quickly, and we can be left wondering what the point of all of this is.

What do Ernest Hemmingway, Marilyn Monroe, Michael Hutchence, Kurt Cobain, Anthony Bourdain, Chris Cornell, Lil' Chris, David Foster Wallace, and Robin Williams all have in common? They each were immense talents and tremendously successful in their lives. But they each committed suicide. They each ended their own lives despite achieving unbelievable success. We of course don't want to oversimplify. There were, no doubt, many contributing factors (for example, mental health, drug addiction, and the like), but it shows that many of us long for more and for something different, even when we have much. We are often tempted to think if we could gain certain things, say, more wealth, then we will be happy. But when we achieve these things, we may very well find ourselves even less satisfied. Even though we spend our days toiling for the promise of these material goods, we know they end in disappointment.

Blaise Pascal once said, "All complain, princes and subjects, noblemen and commoners, old and young, strong and weak, learned and ignorant, healthy and sick, of all countries, all times, all ages, and all conditions."[1] His point is that no matter our station in life, all people find themselves unsatisfied by their lives. We often think things like, *If I can just get that job promotion, then I'll be satisfied.* We may even make an incredible sacrifice of our freedoms and neglect our families and friends to get it. We may work ungodly hours to find success—only to gain it and realize it wasn't all that great. Okay, I guess it's that *next* promotion that will make it all worth it. Kreeft and Tacelli say,

> One may say, "Although I am not perfectly happy now, I believe I would be if only I had ten million dollars, a Lear jet, and a new mistress every day." The reply to this is, of course, "Try it. You won't like it." It's been tried and has never satisfied. In fact, billions of people have performed and are even now performing trillions of such experiments, desperately seeking the ever-elusive satisfaction they crave. For even if they won the whole world, it would not be enough to fill one human heart.[2]

This seems to characterize our lives: always looking forward to what we think will be satisfying but so often being disappointed.

These considerations lead to the curious fact that we all long for something we don't find in this world:

Curious fact 8: We have a desire for something nothing in this world satisfies.

Restless Hearts

Aurelius Augustinus was a bright and extremely talented young man living in the fourth century who had a significant degree of privilege. The man, who would later become known as Saint Augustine, was an example of someone who sought truth and satisfaction, and despite material success found himself with a restless heart. He began his search, like many youths of today, looking for pleasure to satisfy this restless heart. He was especially interested in, well, girls! He liked girls so much that, after he became a Christian, he did not think he'd be able to embrace a chaste life as a priest. He even had a mistress for much of his early years, and they had a child out of wedlock.

Augustine's openness to the Lord first came in his exposure to philosophy. He was reading Cicero's *Hortensius* and observed,

> That book changed my mental attitude, and changed the character of my prayers to Thyself, O Lord. It altered my wishes and my desires. Suddenly, every vain hope became worthless to me and I yearned with unbelievable ardor of heart for the immortality of wisdom. I began to rise up, so that I might return to Thee. . . . The love of wisdom bears the Greek name, philosophy, and it was with this love that that book [*Hortensius*] enkindled me. . . . Since at that time, as thou knowest, O Light of my heart, the words of [Scripture] were unknown to me, I was delighted with Cicero's exhortation, at least enough so that I was stimulated by it, and enkindled and inflamed to love, to seek, to obtain, to hold, and to embrace, not this or that sect, but wisdom itself, wherever it might be.[3]

Unfortunately, this work of Cicero is now lost to us. So we don't know what Augustine saw that altered his wishes and desires, but in reading this philosophical work, Augustine "yearned with unbelievable ardor for the immortality of wisdom." He came to have a taste for truth, and not just any truth but for eternal truth. Augustine came to abandon his pleasure-seeking ways and set his life toward seeking this immortal wisdom.

He turned to both academic achievement and religious pursuits. Here too he found little satisfaction. He followed a religious view called Manichaeism for nearly a decade. But this left him unsatisfied with unanswered questions. It was only after he came to embrace the gospel of Christianity that he felt peace. He proclaims, "You have made us for yourself, O Lord, and our hearts are restless until they rest in You."[4] His restless heart finally found rest, and he came to understand that all of his restlessness was a drive toward finding satisfaction in God.

Infinite Abyss

Fast forward to the seventeenth century. Like Augustine, Blaise Pascal also came to Christ later in life. He was thirty-one years old and had already achieved many accomplishments in math and science. Pascal believed in the truth of Christianity due to something of a conversion experience in his early twenties, but this was largely an intellectual commitment only. Late one night Pascal had a profound spiritual experience that changed his life forever. He turned his efforts from math and science to theology and apologetics. Here, with a genuine relationship with Christ, Pascal found true satisfaction. Pascal writes,

> All men seek happiness. This is without exception. Whatever different means they employ, they all tend to this end. The cause of some going to war, and of others

avoiding it, is the same desire in both, attended with different views. The will never takes the least step but to this object. This is the motive of every action of every man, even of those who hang themselves.[5]

The universal human desire is to seek happiness. But, as Pascal says, we are unable to secure this happiness. All people complain no matter what station in life they occupy. Our lives are marked by a failure to find lasting happiness. He goes on:

What is it then that this desire and this inability proclaim to us, but that there was once in man a true happiness of which there now remain to him only the mark and empty trace, which he in vain tries to fill from all his surroundings, seeking from things absent the help he does not obtain in things present? But these are all inadequate, because the infinite abyss can only be filled by an infinite and immutable object, that is to say, only by God Himself.[6]

For Pascal we have a restless heart because we face an *infinite* abyss in finding satisfaction. And this infinite abyss has something of the trace or shape of God. Many have summarized Pascal's claim here by describing this as a God-shaped hole. As he says, it is an infinite abyss that can only be filled with an infinite object, namely, God himself.

C. S. Lewis's Pursuit

A few centuries later, a man of the twentieth century, C. S. Lewis, also saw his life as on a trajectory to find satisfaction and peace in God. At a relatively young age Lewis enthusiastically embraced atheism. But he also was fascinated by and drawn to myths and fantasies. Lewis was, as an Oxford don, a specialist in English literature with a special interest in pagan mythology. Lewis saw meaning and rich significance in myths, but his atheism told him the world was just not this way. His atheism told him that the world was nothing more than molecules in motion with no meaning, purpose, or value. He says,

> Nearly all that I loved I believed to be imaginary; nearly all that I believed to be real I thought grim and meaningless; I care[d] for nothing but the gods and heroes, the garden of the Hesperides, Launcelot and the Grail but believe[d] in nothing but atoms and evolution and military service.[7]

It wasn't until Lewis's close friends and colleagues J. R. R. Tolkien and Hugo Dyson challenged him with the idea of a "true myth" that Lewis came to open his heart to the Christian claims. Now, we often use the word *myth* to mean false or fictional. But in a technical sense a myth is a story that provides meaning and significance. Most myths are fictional stories, but the thought that intrigued Lewis was that Christianity is a story that provides meaning and significance, just as many myth stories do, but this one is different: it's a story that happened as a genuine historical event. This seemed to click for Lewis. He found the source of what he called "Joy" (with a capital J).

The Argument from Joy

Joy, for Lewis, is not simply happiness or pleasure. It's safe to say that Joy, for Lewis, is not what most of us think of when we think of the emotion of joy. Joy is, for Lewis, actually an *unful-filled* desire. But somewhat paradoxically, it is a pleasurable unfulfilled desire. It is a deep longing that, as Lewis says, "is itself more desirable than any other satisfaction."[8] We are intrinsically drawn to its pursuit even though we are left ultimately unsatisfied in the pursuit of its satisfaction in this life. Robert Holyer has summarized Lewis's notion saying, "There are in effect two essential elements of Joy: a sort of rapturous desire and a sense of being separated or alienated from the object of desire."[9]

We feel Joy in those quiet and reflective moments when life might be quite good, but we wonder if this is all there is. It's the feeling that, as badly as we want certain things (for example, financial security, healthy relationships, career success), nothing in this world will actually satisfy. Lewis believed that this longing ultimately pointed us to something beyond this world, the transcendent. It was an indication that the transcendent exists. Why think this? Lewis pointed out that for every desire we have there is a corresponding object in the world that satisfies that desire. This isn't to say that just because we have a desire for something it must exist. Rather, it is to observe that for any desire that is both natural and general within us, there exist the objects of that desire. Lewis puts it this way, "A baby feels hunger; well, there is such a thing as food. A duckling wants to swim; well, there is such a thing as water. Men feel sexual desire; well, there is such a thing as sex."[10] This, he thought, gave us reason to think that a corresponding object of Joy existed as well.

We may have specific desires for something that does not exist, say, a calorie-free chocolate bar or perhaps we are caught up with the desire to hang out with space aliens. But these are all specific desires of more general categories (for example, hunger or friendship). Calorie-free chocolate bars may not exist, but one may satisfy our hunger or even our desire for a tasty treat by other existing things. Space aliens do not exist, but there are plenty of ways to satisfy our desires to hang out with interesting people.

But when it comes to Joy, this seems to be natural. We come into the world searching for the transcendent and the ultimately meaningful. And yet there is nothing in this world that satisfies this desire. Lewis concludes on the basis of this fact, "If I find in myself a desire which no experience in this world can satisfy, the most probable explanation is that I was made for another world."[11]

Here's how Kreeft and Tacelli lay out the argument from desire:

1. Every natural or innate desire in us points to a corresponding real object that can satisfy the desire.

2. There exists in us a desire that nothing in time, nothing on earth, no creature can satisfy.

3. Therefore, there exists something outside of time, earth, and creatures that can satisfy this desire.[12]

Many people have found this argument quite compelling. Peter Kreeft has said that aside from Anselm's famous ontological argument, this is "the single most intriguing argument in the history of human thought."[13] But just as many have found it uncompelling, especially if they aren't already convinced of the truth of Christianity.

A Compelling Argument?

The problem that many people have with the argument comes in the first premise. The claim generalizes on the fact that most desires we have, have a corresponding object. But the problem is claims such as this can so easily be wrong. You may have met a few Texans and they've all been exceedingly nice. Suppose you generalize that "all Texans are nice." The problem of course is that all it takes is one grumpy Texan and this generalization is false. The critic finds the argument from desire uncompelling because it seems so easy to imagine the possibility that the desire of Joy does not have an object. It could be the case that all our other desires have objects even if the desire for the transcendent does not have an object.

In response, the first thing to point out is that the desire is for something transcendent. So saying we haven't found an object that satisfies the desire for transcendence in our material world does nothing to prove there isn't a being who is transcendent and beyond the material world. We are looking in the wrong place if we are looking into the created world to find the being who would satisfy this transcendent desire.

Second, it's better to understand (and frame) the argument not as a generalization but as an explanatory argument. We have been using explanatory arguments in providing reasons to believe in Christianity. Explanatory arguments go like this: You come across some phenomenon (such as, an odd fact that needs explaining). You will then run through what would best explain the phenomenon and come to what you take to be the best explanation.

Let's say I walk into my house one day after work and my normally busy home is oddly quiet. Usually, my home is abuzz with kids playing, doing homework, practicing gymnastics, or volleyball, and all of this is usually all happening in the living room! But nothing is going on this evening.

Now this odd situation will immediately call for explanation. I'll start wondering what explains the fact that no one's around at what is normally a very busy time. I may quickly consider a few different explanations. Perhaps I think

1. *There is a school program or sporting event I've forgotten about.* But let's say I take a quick look at the calendar on the fridge, which includes all our events, and there's no event for tonight. And so I wonder . . .

2. *They are all in the backyard.* I check this out and see that it is not so. I start to get a little worried and allow myself to wonder more fancifully.

3. *Maybe they've been abducted by aliens.* I realize this is not very spiritual, and I reconsider . . .

4. *The rapture has occurred.*

None of these explanations seem entirely plausible given what I am seeing, but suppose I finally get a bit more evidence and I come to the best explanation. I hear a little giggle behind the couch. I now have the best explanation for why the house is quiet, and I come to this realization moments before my family jumps out from behind the couches screaming "Surprise!"

In this scenario I considered some possible explanations and came to the best explanation given the facts before me. We reason this way all the time. We are constantly attempting to make sense of what's before us. We do this in mundane ways in searching for lost car keys, deciding the best route to work, and cooking a good meal. But we also use this form of reasoning in important matters such as diagnosing a health condition or testing a hypothesis in science.[14] We also should use this form of reasoning to evaluate a worldview, and I think it is best to see the argument from desire in this light.

Explaining Our Desire for the Transcendent

It's a curious fact that we each have a desire for something that nothing in this world satisfies. But what's the best explanation for this fact? It's not plausible to think there is no reason at all for this desire: surely there is some reason for this desire. The most promising options seem to be that either this desire is a product of nature (or perhaps evolution) or it points us to God. How do we decide which of these options is the better explanation?

Perhaps nature or evolution produced this desire in us for some reason that helps us survive in the world. Erik Wielenberg has speculated that this unsatisfied desire for the transcendent has the purpose of driving us to excellence. His thought is that if we had contentment in life, then this would likely lead to stagnation, which is dangerous in the midst of a competition for limited resources necessary for survival. He says, "Evolutionarily speaking, a good strategy is never to be entirely satisfied with one's lot in life. Lasting contentment breeds inaction, which in turn breeds reproductive failure—at least when the competition is not entirely content."[15] If we are unsatisfied by life no matter what earthly goods we have, then this drives us to never rest content, which, Wielenberg claims, would be a clear evolutionary advantage.

Now Wielenberg recognizes the fact that someone may object to this explanation as a "just so story." That is, it is an explanation that is merely possible but lacks any further evidence. And Wielenberg recognizes that he has provided no further evidence for his evolutionary explanation. However, he argues that in the present context this point is not damaging. The reason is that he thinks the theistic explanation of Joy lacks empirical evidence as well. What we have are essentially two competing "just so stories." If this is right, then we have a stalemate. And a stalemate in this context means failure for the argument from desire, which is supposed to provide some positive reason to believe that a transcendent object exists.[16]

In response to Wielenberg we may concede the stalemate but deny that this means failure for the argument from desire. The reason for this is it is not necessarily intended as a standalone positive reason to believe in God. As I presented it, it is intended to be part of a cumulative case of curious facts that are all explained by Christian theism.

To illustrate, suppose Smith is on trial for bank robbery. Police detectives have found Smith's DNA at the scene of the crime. Smith also fits the description an eyewitness has given who watched the entire robbery. But the eyewitness couldn't be sure it was Smith. Jones also fits the description, so there's something of a stalemate here. If all the jury had to go on was the eyewitness testimony, then the stalemate means we can't rationally believe that Smith is guilty. But the fact that Smith fits the description of the bank robber plus the fact that his DNA was found at the scene of the crime combines for cumulative force. While it by itself is not conclusive, it does add to the cumulative weight of the evidence despite its being a stalemate on this specific front.

Christian theism also seems far more preferable than the evolutionary picture. To affirm the evolutionary explanation is to affirm that life is ultimately unsatisfying. But then this is stagnating and completely defeats our motivation for seeking satisfaction in life. To accept Wielenberg's explanation is to recognize that Joy is never satisfied. But then what does this view have to say to a person who is dissatisfied in life? All it can say is "Accept this fact and get on with it." If it's truly a stalemate, the theistic picture is the preferable one.

But I see no reason to concede the stalemate. The empirical evidence is the fact that all other desires have corresponding objects, which suggests the desire for transcendence has a corresponding object as well. And again there is a great variety of reasons to think that Christian theism is true. The Christian theistic explanation is a single thesis that makes good sense of a variety of curious facts. The evolutionary explanation of Joy does not have reasons such as this to think it is true. It is "just so" in a way that the theistic picture is not. This seems to provide a compelling reason (again, not proof) to think we are made for another world.

The Paradox of Pleasure Seeking

Many religions picture the ultimate satisfaction of desire as some ultimate state of pleasure. The way some religions put it is that if we fulfill certain religious obligations, then we'll find ourselves in a paradise filled with an array of pleasures. But, as we close this chapter, I'd like to suggest we are not ultimately designed for pleasure and that pleasure seeking leads to our misery.

This is sometimes called the paradox of hedonism (i.e., pleasure seeking). We might be tempted to think the hedonist or the pleasure-seeker should be the happiest person around. After all, this person is constantly seeking and experiencing pleasure. But the reality is that this person is often the most miserable around. This is because pleasure is always fleeting and often leaves us with greater desire and less satisfaction. Parties aren't supposed to last all day and every day. They are fun when they are rare and special. When every day is a party, then we end up miserable. When we overdo any immediate pleasure, we are left miserable and longing for another hit of satisfaction. This is certainly true of illicit drugs and alcohol abuse. But this is also true of overdoing movie watching, video game playing, junk food, sweets, and so on.

The paradox then is that pleasure seeking is the best way to be miserable. It's only when we don't specifically seek pleasure that we may find it. We have to instead seek after worthy ends such as serving and helping people. It's worth pausing to catch the irony here. The best way to live a happy life is to make your life all about serving people. When we live selfishly in trying to make ourselves happy, we rarely succeed.

Jesus put it this way, "Whoever finds their life will lose it, and whoever loses their life for my sake will find it" (Matthew 10:39). In the context of this passage Jesus is speaking about the cost of discipleship. We often think we need to focus our lives on living happy and getting as much stuff as we can. But to live selfishly for ourselves is ultimately for us to lose our lives. This is because we would be hoping in this life only. We would be putting all of our chips on this temporary existence instead of having eternal hope. We, like the pleasure-seeker, are only seeking what's relatively immediate. However, if we lose our life (that is, fully submit ourselves to Jesus in discipleship), then we will find it in our eternal hope. It's the ultimate long game.

C. S. Lewis makes the point that pleasure-seekers do not need to tamp down their desires and settle for less. Rather, their desire is much too shortsighted. Lewis says:

> Our Lord finds our desires not too strong, but too weak. We are half-hearted creatures, fooling about with drink and sex and ambition when infinite joy is offered us, like an ignorant child who wants to go on making mud pies in a slum because he cannot imagine what is meant by the offer of a holiday at the sea. We are far too easily pleased.[17]

We need then to set our sights on the transcendent. Our desire for Joy is the way for genuine happiness. If we are designed for something beyond this world, then we ought to set ourselves to finding our satisfaction with the only thing that can fit the infinite abyss, namely, the infinite God himself.

Walking Off a Broken Leg

But something stands in our way of finding satisfaction and rest in God: there is something deeply wrong with us. Occasionally, someone might express the belief that people are on the whole good. However, with only a little prodding, most will admit that despite our best intentions everyone makes mistakes along the way, some of which have terrible consequences. So, we have a problem, and we spend a fortune and countless hours in therapy, on self-help tools, and religious efforts as a corrective to this problem. Christianity offers a solution to this problem. Christianity is not simply the better solution to our human predicament than the alternatives. Instead, Christianity is the only solution that actually addresses our human predicament.

We won't be able to canvass the many and various proposed solutions offered by religious traditions. It's possible, however, to capture a wide range of these claims where the solution has crucially to do with *doing* something. Here the religious person prescribes certain religious practices, prayers, or prostrations that somehow make us right with a divine reality or in an otherwise enlightened state. But why should performing certain actions solve our moral depravity? To see the problem here, consider the fact that the human predicament we were trying to solve had to do with failing to do the morally right actions in the first place. The relevant question is how does providing a list of further actions even address that problem? If we couldn't live appropriately before, it seems highly unlikely that we will do better with a new list of things to do.

Here's an analogy. Suppose you've had a bad fall, experience tremendous pain, and therefore suspect that you have broken your leg. You go to your doctor, and suppose he says, "My diagnosis is that it is indeed a traumatic fracture of the femur bone." Still in serious pain, you seek to come to grips with what this will mean for you, and he says, "My prescribed solution is to just go ahead walk it off." Ridiculous, right? The problem of course is that you went to the doctor because you had a problem related to walking to start with, and being told to walk it off simply doesn't address the problem. In fact, it is certain to exacerbate the problem.

In the moral case, we are unable to live well in our current condition, and so being told to do certain things does not seem to even address the problem. We can't seem to do the right things, so how does being told to do certain right things help solve our predicament? With this in mind, just think about how hollow it rings to be told to recite certain prescribed prayers or to fulfill your two-year missionary service or pray toward the east *for the purpose of* solving what's wrong with us. This is not to say that all religious *doings* are in themselves wrong. Nor that religious works aren't powerful and beneficial in various ways. The point is, rather, that the works themselves don't address our human condition. There must be something at the core of the prescription that addresses what's wrong with us.

By contrast to these, the Christian solution does uniquely address our human condition. However, before I offer a statement of this, it's worth mentioning that we Christians have unfortunately so often fallen into the temptation of making ours a solution of religious doings. We virtually make idols out of things like spiritual disciplines, church attendance, evange-listic efforts, and a host of other things we think earn us some degree of right standing with God. Again, religious perfor-mances are not unimportant. Indeed, our faith is dead without them (James 2:17). However, it is not what we do and how we perform that saves. If it was, then let's face it, we would be in deep trouble!

There is perhaps no more profound truth in the history of religious and philosophical thought than Paul's statement: "It is by grace you have been saved, through faith—and this is not from yourselves, it the gift of God—not by works, so that no one can boast" (Ephesians 2:8-9). There is no other religion in the history of the world that ever predicated salvation on grace through faith. The Christian gospel doesn't tell us to stop being desperately sick and corrupt by performing a list of particular deeds. It in fact tells us to give up on this hopeless pursuit and be made right by the work of Christ, as we make him Lord.

Not only does this desire—our restlessness, the infinite abyss in our hearts, and Lewis's Joy—point to the existence of God, this God-shaped desire can be filled, and our desire for the transcendent can be satisfied. But not by our works and our doing. It's only through *his doing*—that is, Christ's work on the cross—that our human condition is addressed, as we surrender and place faith in him.

Is the God of the Bible Good and Loving?

For God is good—or rather,
of all goodness He is the Fountainhead.

ATHANASIUS

There would be no manifestation of God's grace or true goodness,
if there was no sin to be pardoned, no misery to be saved from.

JONATHAN EDWARDS

The Bible may, indeed does, contain a warrant for trafficking
in humans, for ethnic cleansing, for slavery, for bride-price,
and for indiscriminate massacre, but we are not bound
by any of it because it was put together by crude,
uncultured human mammals.

CHRISTOPHER HITCHENS

We've looked at eight curious facts that provide reasons to believe in Christianity. We turn now to ask some big questions that challenge this belief. Once again, we cannot canvass all the many possible challenges we may have. The goal here is to consider a few difficult questions to model how to navigate big questions as they come. We begin by asking if the God of the Bible is good and loving.

The Bible doesn't often pull punches but rather describes life as it really is. The narratives are often not rated G. In fact, at times they probably wouldn't be rated PG or even PG-13. There's murder, rape, sexual affairs, violent battles, theft, lying, and treachery. Since the Bible details the lives of sinners, this is to be expected. Even the greatest heroes of the Bible (except of course the greatest hero, Jesus) are flawed. King David, for example, is a man after God's own heart. But he was guilty of both adultery and premeditated murder!

But when it comes to the God of the Bible, we are dealing with a being who is seen as perfectly loving and good. At times we expect imperfect humans to do terrible things. But, in the Christian view, God is perfectly good. But here's the undeniable reality. God sometimes commands and even himself causes wide-scale bloodshed.

Much of the focus here will be on the Old Testament accounts of this sort. Richard Dawkins says,

> The God of the Old Testament is arguably the most unpleasant character in all fiction: jealous and proud of it; a petty, unjust, unforgiving control-freak; a vindictive, bloodthirsty ethnic cleanser; a misogynistic, homophobic, racist, infanticidal, genocidal, filicidal, pestilential, megalomaniacal, sadomasochistic, capriciously malevolent bully.[1]

This is not really an argument, of course. It's simply a claim. But rhetorically speaking, it's a gut punch. In a single soundbite-sized sentence, it raises a slew of challenges, and none of them can be answered with a corresponding soundbite or simple quip. We won't be able to meet every challenge Dawkins raises and will instead boil it down into a single challenge. If God is good and loving, why does God command and even commit violence and killing?

God Commands the Killing of People Groups

We have to be honest. A cursory reading of books like Joshua or Judges gives a variety of instances of divinely sanctioned battles and bloody conflicts. God commands Joshua and his armies to take the land of Canaan for their own. The Israelites understood the land of Canaan to be rightfully theirs as the Promised Land, promised by God. Israel marches against these Canaanites and surrounding people to repossess the land in conquest, which at times is violent and bloody. After they possess the land, Israel continues to struggle against surrounding nations, which sometimes prompts violent responses. All of this seemingly has the blessing of God.

So there is no way around this fact. God does command the killing of large groups of people. For example, God commands Israel,

> Completely destroy them—the Hittites, Amorites, Canaanites, Perizzites, Hivites and Jebusites—as the Lord your God has commanded you. Otherwise, they will teach you to follow all the detestable things they do in worshiping their gods, and you will sin against the Lord your God. (Deuteronomy 20:17-18)

Perhaps the most explicitly shocking charge comes in 1 Samuel 15:3. In the passage Samuel the prophet says to Saul, "Now go, attack the Amalekites and totally destroy all that belongs to them. Do not spare them; put to death men and women, children and infants, cattle and sheep, camels and donkeys." How could these be the commands of a good and loving God?

Hyperbolic Language?

How can we make sense of these passages?

One possible response is that these commands need to be put into the context of the time. There is evidence to suggest that when using battle language, it was common to overstate the situation in terms of total annihilation when the reality was it was much more limited in actuality.

For example, Joshua 10:40 states, "Joshua subdued the whole region, including the hill country, the Negev, the western foothills and the mountain slopes, together with all their kings. He left no survivors. He totally destroyed all who breathed, just as the LORD, the God of Israel, had commanded."

However, as we continue through Scripture, it is obvious this total annihilation did not occur. As we read on, we see plenty of these people still very much alive. Could Joshua have simply gotten this wrong? It's not likely such an egregious inconsistency would be made.

A more plausible reading is that the language is hyperbolic (that is, exaggerated). Paul Copan says, "Joshua used the rhetorical bravado language of his day, asserting that all the land was captured, all the kings defeated, and all the Canaanites destroyed. . . . [when] Joshua himself acknowledged that this wasn't literally so."[2] For example, in Joshua 10:36-39, it describes a total annihilation of Hebron and Debir. Joshua "left no survivors. . . . They totally destroyed [Hebron] and everyone in it" (v. 37), and "They . . . put them to the sword. Everyone in it they totally destroyed. They left no survivors. They did to Debir and its king as they had done to . . . Hebron" (v. 39). Sounds like total annihilation, right? The problem is that Joshua is clear a few chapters later that these towns were not totally annihilated. Joshua 15:13-15 describes and even names inhabitants that were still there at both Hebron and Debir. These would be such egregious contradictions that it's implausible to think these are just overlooked mistakes.

Copan makes the point that this is a common way people talked about battles in the surrounding cultures. Many times in ancient Near Eastern literature total annihilation is claimed even though we know it did not happen. An example of this comes from the Merneptah Stele, an Egyptian tablet that records Egypt's conflicts with Israel. On it Pharaoh Merneptah claims, "Israel is laid waste and his seed is not." We of course know this wasn't true. It's hyperbolic language intended to, in a way, cheer on their military exploits. This seems similar to the way the book of Joshua makes these sweeping claims of total annihilation and yet at the end of the book of Joshua there is a warning against associating with and especially intermarrying with these very same nations (Joshua 23:12-13).

This would be like the hyperbolic language we use in talking about sports. Suppose a coach enthusiastically said, "Okay, team, get out there and utterly destroy them!" The team would likely understand that this is not to be taken literally. The coach means they are to play to win big. But of course, good coaches teach their players to win only within the rules of the game. In the same way there is a plausible case to be made that the Israelites understood these commands in light of the rest of God's law, and killing noncombatant civilians was certainly outside of God's law. If God had literally commanded the killing of men, women, and children, then we'd expect to see some accounts detailing these massacres. But this is precisely what we don't see. The details we get always concern the fighting of combatants.

We might wonder why they would talk this way if it was not meant to be taken literally. And here the answer is that we don't know. Idioms are funny things. Consider how strange it would sound to someone from another culture if they heard us say that it's "raining cats and dogs" or that "the kids are bouncing off the walls" or some task is a "piece of cake." People would likely think we are crazy, but we don't even notice how extreme they sound because they are so familiar, and yet we know exactly what they mean. The point is there's no easy answer for why we say "it's raining cats and dogs" rather than just saying that it is raining hard.

Copan suggests that this annihilation language was a common way people talked in their day. It was understood to be bravado and a way to emphasize dominance in a battle.

While this is a possible answer and may be genuinely helpful for some instances of violence in Scripture, this isn't a completely satisfying answer for me. After all, it appears that God is commanding extreme violence even if not total annihilation.

A loving and good God commanding partial annihilation seems to be problem enough.

Did God Commit the Mass Killing of People?

It's also important to see that God also directly causes the killing of people. The most obvious example of this is Noah's flood of Genesis 6–9, where God says, "I will wipe from the face of the earth the human race I have created—and with them the animals, the birds and the creatures that move along the ground" (Genesis 6:7) except for Noah and his family. This, it seems, is an instance of total annihilation. There's no possibility of hyperbolic language, and it is a horrifying passage of Scripture. There's a fair amount of irony in the fact that we often decorate our children's nurseries with a Noah and the ark theme given that this is an event in which most of the population of the earth, both humans and animals, are completely wiped out. Even if one thought that the hyperbolic-language strategy was satisfying in commanding bloodshed, that strategy doesn't apply here with this.

It's easy to see why people struggle with stories such as this. Again, how could the act of directly wiping out the population of the planet be the action of a good and loving God?

To respond to this very difficult challenge we first must make clear that the reality of Noah's flood is not pleasant. As I mentioned in chapter five, we do not have to like a story such as this (and I don't), even if we think God is completely justified in his actions and the passage is entirely true (as I do). To be clear, the account of Noah's Ark is rich with meaning and crucially important to the overall story arc of Scripture, but even so, the judgment portions of the narrative are harsh and rather unpleasant.

But being a harsh and unpleasant reality doesn't itself present a problem for God's being good and loving. What we need to determine is whether God is morally wrong in this action. Life has its unpleasant realities that are not morally wrong. Consider the damage caused by a surgeon when someone has open-heart surgery. The details of this surgery are an extremely unpleasant reality. Most of us would not be able to stomach watching it being performed. There is a long and extremely painful recovery for this surgery, and the person may never get back to full health. But this does not make the actions of the surgeon morally wrong. Even though it is an unpleasant reality, surgery may be the only way to save the person's life!

War is also an unpleasant reality. Upward of eighty million people died in World War II! The horrors experienced by our soldiers are almost unbelievable. But this doesn't make the men and women who fought morally wrong. They were called on to do many horrifying but morally justified things to stop the Axis powers. Enforcement of laws and the protection of people will also often involve violence and harm. Unpleasant? Yes. Morally wrong? Not when acted on in morally appropriate and justified ways.

Evaluating Moral Acts

With any act of harm we really can't evaluate the morality of it without knowing the context. We need to know two things. First, we have to know who is acting and whether the person causing the harm has the relevant authority. And, second, we have to know whether there is a justifying purpose for causing the harm. In my earlier example it is a surgeon trained to perform open-heart surgery. The point and purpose of the surgery is to save the life of the person with heart problems. And a surgeon would have the authority to perform the surgery because the hospital is the appropriate body authorizing such surgeries when the person elects to have it performed. Harm is certainly caused in open-heart surgery, but it is justified harm.

How about Noah's flood? What is the point or purpose of the flood? To answer this question we must see who the major actors are in the narrative.

First, let's look at the people. Genesis 6 is very explicit about what the people were like. Here's how Genesis 6 describes the people:

- The LORD saw how great the wickedness of the human race had become on the earth, and that every inclination of the thoughts of the human heart was only evil all the time. (v. 5)
- The earth was corrupt in God's sight and was full of violence. (v. 11)
- All the people on earth had corrupted their ways. (v. 12)
- The earth [was] filled with violence. (v. 13)

According to the narrative the people of the earth were utterly wicked to the extent that every inclination was completely evil all the time!

The other character in the narrative is God. Who is God as pictured in the Bible? God is pictured as loving and good.

Perhaps the most explicit statement of this is in 1 John 4, where the phrase "God is love" is used twice (vv. 8, 16).

So, God is love, but it would be unfair to the biblical picture to think that God is *only* love. The Bible also clearly pictures God as holy and just. In fact, there are many more verses throughout the Bible affirming the holiness and justice of God than there are of the love of God.

Here's just a sampling:

- There is no one holy like the LORD. (1 Samuel 2:2)
- Be holy because I, the LORD your God, am holy. (Leviticus 19:2)
- Holy, holy, holy is the LORD Almighty; the whole earth is full of his glory! (Isaiah 6:3)
- Just as he who called you is holy, so be holy in all you do. (1 Peter 1:15)
- God will bring every deed into judgment, including every hidden thing, whether it is good or evil. (Ecclesiastes 12:14)
- Just as people are destined to die once, and after that to face judgment. (Hebrews 9:27)

The point is that though God is indeed good and loving, he's also holy and just and therefore the judge of humanity. And God's goodness and his justice go hand in hand.

To see this, let's say a man commits a grievous crime. He comes before the judge who says, "You are free to go." Let's say the man goes out and commits a similar grievous crime, and the judge again lets him go free. And this happens a third, fourth, and fifth time. Is this judge good? No, this judge seems downright evil allowing these injustices to go unpunished and allowing further injustice to occur. The judge, in a way, has become a party to these crimes. A good judge is just and doesn't let moral wrong go unpunished. If God is perfectly good, then he *must* justly punish sin.

Genesis 6 makes clear that it was the extreme wickedness of the people ('every inclination of the thoughts of the human heart was only evil all the time') that precipitated God's judgment. It's not as if the people of the earth were innocent do-gooders and God became unjustifiably angry with them. According to the narrative at hand the people were extremely wicked and thereby deserved judgment. And it's really important we stick with the narrative, since it's the narrative that's at issue. The claim is that God cannot be good and loving judging the people the way he did in the flood account. But if the people were extremely wicked and God is the righteous judge of humanity, then he had the authority to carry out justice.

Similar considerations apply to the Canaanite people and the surrounding cultures. They were extremely wicked. Similar to the judgment in the flood account, the situation is not one in which God's people are mounting attacks on innocent and peace-loving people. These people were engaged in a host of evil practices, including child sacrifice. Deuteronomy 12:31 says, "They practice every detestable act, which the LORD hates, for their gods. They even burn their sons and daughters in the fire to their gods" (CSB). The thought here is that it's at least possible the people had grown to be so utterly wicked that Israel was dealing with them harshly in proportion to their wickedness. It wouldn't do to simply exhort them to stop sacrificing their children any more than it would have to tell Hitler and the Third Reich to please stop gassing innocent people in the Nazi Holocaust. The extreme wickedness of the Holocaust called for a bloody war to destroy this evil force, and there were unfortunate causalities along the way. This is no doubt also the case with the Canaanite conquest.

Does God Have the Right to Take Life?

There are likely many follow-up questions here. For example, did God have to punish by such an extreme measure as bloody war or by a flood? And was everybody who suffered in the judgment wicked to such a degree they deserved to die?

These are extremely difficult questions, and we don't have space to fully address all of these issues. And the reality is that we may not have fully satisfying answers for some of these questions. I find the above helpful for addressing some of these difficult concerns. But questions remain. Since we are not aiming at certainty, I don't need to know why God chose to use a flood to wipe out humanity in the judgment of wickedness. It's not for me to say that he should have used a more pleasant method. What's important is we see that a narrative like this doesn't entail that God is unjust or evil. Judgment—even extreme judgment—of sin is justified.

Moreover, it's worth keeping in mind that according to Scripture, God is in charge of this world. God brings the world into being and sustains every particle into being at every moment that it exists. God also directs the course of history in his sovereignty. This means that God's purposes and perspective extend far beyond what we see in a particular event at a particular time. Thus, God has justifying reasons we simply can't fathom. So while I don't have all the answers here, I think I know enough to rationally believe that God, in his goodness and love and his holiness and justice, has justifying reasons for commanding and committing the violence we see in the Old Testament.

Will these responses satisfy the committed unbeliever? Probably not. But, just to remind ourselves, this is not our aim. We aim to ask the question and consider what we can say in response. Though many questions remain, I don't think this problem entails that God is evil. It's plausible that God has justified reasons for the harsh judgments in these narratives even if we don't know what all those reasons are. These are certainly unpleasant passages. But it takes more than that to show that the God of the Bible is not good.

Why Is There So Much Pain
and Suffering?

Is [God] willing to prevent evil, but not able? then is he impotent.

Is he able, but not willing? then is he malevolent.

Is he both able and willing? whence then is evil?

DAVID HUME

Naked I came from my mother's womb,

and naked shall I return.

The LORD gave, and the LORD has taken away;

blessed be the name of the LORD.

JOB (ESV)

The great gift of Easter is hope—Christian hope which makes us

have that confidence in God, in his ultimate triumph, and in his

goodness and love, which nothing can shake.

BASIL HUME

The question of God's action in the Old Testament brings up a more fundamental question. The challenge of chapter ten was whether God's love and goodness are consistent with certain passages involving violence and death. The challenge we'll consider in this chapter has to do more broadly with whether God's goodness and power are consistent with the existence of wide-scale pain and suffering. This is, in many ways, the most pressing question for believing in the existence of God. The thought is that if God is good, loves us, and has all power, then there shouldn't be so much pain and suffering. But there is a seemingly extravagant amount of pain and suffering. Here's a big question: Does evil, pain, and suffering suggest there is no God?

The Problem of Evil

The reason that pain and suffering is an especially difficult problem is that there's so much of it and no one is completely immune. Perhaps if there was just a small amount we could make sense of why God would allow it. But it only takes a moment to think of the last heart-wrenching tragedy to which the media machine has forced our undivided attention. And for some of us, the pain and suffering are right there in our midst. At times we are going about our merry way and suddenly suffering shows up.

Now no one wants pain and suffering in their world. But what exactly is the problem? Pain and suffering wouldn't be a problem for believing in certain versions of God or gods. If God can do evil, then evil, pain, and suffering are not a problem. The Greek gods, for example, do evil from time to time. They were often interfering with the affairs of people for nefarious reasons. Causing pain and suffering is part of the package when it comes to the Greek gods. So evil is not a problem for the Greek gods.

But, from the Christian view, God is perfectly righteous and is perfectly powerful. God is completely sovereign over all things. Why would a God who is perfectly good and perfectly powerful allow so much pain and suffering? It's natural to think that if there's a God, the world should be far better than it is. Thus, pain and suffering are put forward as disconfirming evidence for the existence of a good, loving, and all-powerful God.

Consider a loving parent. As a parent I do whatever I can to prevent the pain and suffering of my kids. I don't need to be a helicopter parent to care about preventing my child from experiencing unnecessary harm. If my child is chasing after a ball that's gone across a busy highway, I don't simply allow her to run after it. If I did, I would not be good. In fact, if I stood by and let my child run across a busy highway, we might consider me to be downright evil. And God doesn't have the limitations that I do. And yet God seemingly allows us to run across the busy highways of life. More generally, God allows tragic things to happen that he, in his power, has the ability to prevent.

Greater Goods

It is sometimes argued that there must be pain and suffering in the world for God to bring about greater good. For example, I have taught each of my four children how to ride a bicycle. For each of them I would take off the training wheels, get them on the bike, and then hold the handlebar as they pedaled down the street. At a young age kids only have one speed: fast! So I would run at top speed trying to keep them from leaning to one side or another. But at some point I had to let go of the handlebar and just let them ride on their own. If I didn't, they wouldn't have learned to ride a bike. I would have been their life-sized training wheels running all over town! For them to learn to ride a bike on their own, they needed me to let go.

With each of our kids, when I let go, they inevitably fell and perhaps scraped a knee or elbow. Did this make me a bad parent? No, since the only way to completely prevent the possibility of their falling would have prevented them from this greater good, which was learning to ride a bike on their own. A few scrapes and bruises and a few tears seem well worth the great good of kid mobility. Allowing them to experience some pain and suffering wasn't wrong because I had good and justifying reasons for this.

If God has good and justifying reasons for allowing pain and suffering, then God is, in a way, off the hook. If God allows us to suffer for some greater good, then the suffering is similarly justified. But life can often feel like the pain and suffering we go through is completely senseless. People, at no fault of their own, get hurt or sick with a disease and die. There seems to be no greater good that comes in a wide variety of cases. It would be like taking my kids to the biggest and baddest hill in town to learn to ride a bike. Imagine I popped the training wheels off, put them on the bike, and gave them a push down this terrifying hill. It's almost certain that they would get hurt and likely get hurt badly. You might wonder why I would go to the biggest, baddest hill in town to teach my kids to ride a bike. And that's the point. There seems to be no good reason to do this and many compelling reasons to *not* do this. If I were to do this, it would show me to be not good.

The issue comes down to whether God has good and justifying reasons for allowing the pain and suffering we see in the world.

The Free Will Factor

There was a time when certain versions of the so-called problem of evil were taken to be knock-down, drag-out arguments against the existence of God. The basic claim was that evil and God were logically incompatible. That is, if God exists, then evil does not exist because God, being good and all-powerful, would only create a world without any evil at all. The thought was that there is no way both evil and God could be the case, and since obviously there's evil, there must not be a God.

But there has been a complete reversal on this version of the argument (which rarely happens in philosophy!), where even many atheists will admit that this form of the argument is no good. As it turns out, it is just too strong. The claim of the argument amounts to saying there is no conceivable way in which any instances of evil and God could both be the case.

What has convinced many thinkers is that free choice is a good that is only achievable by allowing for the possibility of evil. This is referred to as the *free will defense*.[1] Let's suppose Tom has a girlfriend named Emily. Let's also suppose things are going well for Tom and Emily until he finds out that Emily is being paid off by his parents to date Tom. Yikes! Their whole relationship, he comes to conclude, is a fraud. Why? It's because Emily isn't freely choosing to be with Tom out of love for him; she's in it for the money. Suppose we make it even worse and say Emily is being blackmailed by

Tom's parents to date him. Now, she is being forced to be with him. Doesn't it seem to be of a far greater value for Tom to be with someone who *freely chooses* to love him? But with freedom of choice comes a great risk. There is now the possibility of choosing otherwise.

God could have created us with no free will at all. We could just robotically sing his praises and mechanically follow his wishes all day long. This would be a world without evil, but it would be a world without genuine love too. Forced love, if we think about it, is not love at all. Real love requires choice. And it has seemed to many philosophers that it is better to have a world in which people freely choose to worship and love God than a world in which there is no choice at all.

But here's the thing. If God creates free creatures, then he thereby allows for the possibility of those creatures choosing to do evil. The moment there is genuine freedom is when there's the possibility of doing evil. Thus, it is not the case that God and evil are logically incompatible, because God could have good reasons to allow some evil, namely, a genuine love relationship with you and me.

While this helps with understanding why God may allow some evil, it doesn't explain why there is so much of it. It doesn't explain what looks like senseless pain and suffering. Again, some pain and suffering may seem necessary for securing greater good, but the thought is that surely not every instance of pain and suffering is necessary. What about pain and suffering that is not the result of a free choice? There are things like natural disasters and diseases that are not due to the choices of those individuals affected by them.

We've zeroed in on one of the most difficult problems of all. It seems that God and senseless pain and suffering are at odds. And there's so much pain and suffering in the world that it seems some of it (perhaps much of it) is senseless. Surely, an all-good God would not allow pain and suffering to be heaped on for no reason at all.

But let's challenge this idea. Let's doubt our doubt. From the fact that we don't see the reason, it doesn't follow there is no reason. This brings us to the life of Job.

Job's Struggles

Job is a book filled with wrestling, questions, and struggle. Again, the Bible often presents a very realistic picture of its characters, and Job is no exception. The book details Job's attempt to make sense of a situation of extreme suffering where he has lost his family, his livelihood, and his health.

In the book, Job has a limited perspective. We know more about his situation than Job does because we know that, according to the narrative, Satan requested to afflict Job with intense suffering to test Job's faithfulness to God (Job 1–2). Job is of course oblivious to this fact. From Job's perspective all of his children and his household are killed except he and his wife, he's stripped of his wealth, and he's afflicted with boils, all in short order. Most of the book is occupied with an extended discussion about why this happened. Job has a few "friends" who attempt to explain why Job finds himself in these dire conditions, often accusing him of sin. The overall idea is that Job must have done something to deserve these things. Job thinks he's innocent and cries out to God in despair.

In Job 7:20, he says to God "Why have you made me your target?" In an important passage a bit later in the book, Job cries out, "Though He slay me, I will hope in Him" (Job 13:15 NASB). This is a beautiful picture of his unwavering faith, but not one without questions, struggles, and doubts. Job even adds this, "Nevertheless I will argue my ways before Him" and proceeds to lay out his case for his innocence. The point is Job had placed his hope and trust in God but continued to wrestle with what was to him an undeserved situation.

From the perspective we have, Job is actually right. He was not going through this suffering because of sin in his life. In fact, he was going through this extreme trial because of his faithfulness! Satan wagered that Job was only faithful due to his wealth and ease of life circumstances.

What's interesting is that though Job is right that his trials were not because of sinfulness, God never tells him this. Even at the end of the book, God never answers his questions. God could have let him in on what was going on in the heavenly background, but he doesn't. From Job's perspective his suffering was senseless. But this doesn't mean from God's perspective it was senseless. Why did Job suffer? Well, it's not easy to say. Perhaps the better question is why God allowed Satan to inflict Job with suffering. Again, these are "why" questions that probably won't get a satisfying answer.

What we do see is a difference of vantage points. Our vantage point is always extremely limited, where God's is not. The reason for this is that we occupy a very limited perspective from a tiny slice of history. We can barely discern the intentions of people we know extremely well (even when we are married to them!). So how could we possibly aspire to know whether God, who knows the end from the beginning, allowed certain events for good reasons? It seems we are simply not in a position to say that something is genuinely senseless. It may seem senseless, but it doesn't follow that it is genuinely senseless. It is always possible that God does have good and justifying reasons for the pain and suffering in the world, even if we don't know what those are.

God Has His Reasons

But the mere possibility that God has good and justifying reasons is not very satisfying. It seems we need reason to trust that God has good and justifying reasons even if we don't know what they are.

Do we have reason to trust that God has good and justifying reasons? In a sense the answer is a resounding yes. Again, we may not know the specific reasons why we are going through a specific instance of pain and suffering, but it seems we do have reasons to think that these experiences are not senseless. Why? It's because we have reason independent of the pain and suffering in the world to believe that God is there and that God is good. If we have good reason to believe that God exists, then we have good reason to believe that there isn't senseless evil.

Let's look again at the story of Job. Job never gets the answers he was seeking. But he got something much more powerful than that. At the end of the book God himself shows up, as it says, "from the whirlwind" (Job 38:1 CSB). Even though, for all we know, Job never finds out why he suffered, he does not doubt that God is there and is in complete control of all things. Peter Kreeft says,

> He came. He entered space and time and suffering. He came, like a lover. Love seeks above all intimacy, presence, togetherness. Not happiness. "Better unhappy with her than happy without her"—that is the word of a lover. He came. That is the salient fact, the towering truth, that alone keeps us from putting a bullet through our heads. He came. Job is satisfied even though the God who came gave him absolutely no answers at all to his thousand tortured questions. He did the most important thing and he gave the most important gift: himself.[2]

The thought here is that Job learns that God has a purpose for all the circumstances of life and all the pain and suffering that we go through, even though we won't typically know what those purposes are. We can trust that God is doing a work even when it doesn't make sense to us.

We often *want* to know answers to our why questions, and this is completely natural, but we don't *need* to know. We do need to know God is there in the midst of those questions. We need to know that God is in control and has a purpose for everything. And we need to know that he is good. He may not show up quite the way he did with Job from the whirlwind, but we can know he is there. How? This goes back to the many reasons we have for God, some of which we canvassed in chapter seven. We can know with confidence that God is there and if a God of this sort exists, then we thereby have confidence that God has good and justifying reasons for all the pain and suffering we see.

The Cross

As a final thought, it seems the assumption implied in many of the discussions about the problem of evil is that God owes us a relatively pain-free life. But why think God owes this to us? Why think God is obligated to make our lives more pleasurable than they are?

I see no reason at all to think God owes us a pleasurable life. This is especially true given the fact that we live in a fallen world of which God is the holy judge. On what basis can we demand more ease and comfort in this life as fallen human beings? God does give us good things, but he is not obligated to.

In life, God has our well-being in mind. He doesn't necessarily have our comfort and pleasure as his aim. These are fundamentally different aims. And let's not forget that God has given us redemption as the ultimate gift. The ultimate evidence that God has our well-being in mind is Jesus' work on the cross. Peter Kreeft says,

> How to get God off the hook? God's answer is Jesus. Jesus is not God off the hook but God on the hook. That's why the doctrine of the divinity of Christ is crucial: If that is not God there on the cross but only a good man, then God is not on the hook, on the cross, in our suffering. And if God is not on the hook, then God is not off the hook.[3]

So here's the picture. We are fallen, and we live in a fallen world. Pain and suffering are part of this picture. God doesn't put us through pain and suffering capriciously and for no reason. Even if we don't know what those reasons are, we have plenty of reasons to believe that God is just and good. But it doesn't stop there. God entered this fallen world as one of us to solve the problem of evil. He died on the cross to address evil and sin. He rose from the dead to defeat death.

The ultimate answer to the problem of pain and suffering is Christ crucified and raised in victory. Our ultimate need is not less pain and more pleasure and comfort. Our ultimate need is to find peace with God. This provides hope no matter our circumstances. With this hope we can face down the trials of life that inevitably come. We may not understand all of what is going on with these trials, but they shouldn't lead us away from God. We should run into his loving arms.

Why Isn't God More Obvious?

If I go up to the heavens, you are there;
if I make my bed in the depths, you are there.
If I rise on the wings of the dawn,
if I settle on the far side of the sea,
even there your hand will guide me,
your right hand will hold me fast.

PSALM 139:8-10

My claim, then, is that divine silence might just be an expression
of God's preferred mode of interaction, and that we need not
experience his silence as *absence*.

MICHAEL REA

A god who is all-knowing and all powerful and who does not
even make sure his creatures understand his intention—could
that be a god of goodness? Who allows countless doubts and
dubieties to persist, for thousands of years, as though the salvation
of mankind were unaffected by them, and who on the other
hand holds out the prospect of frightful consequences if any
mistake is made as to the nature of truth?

FRIEDRICH NIETZSCHE

Famed twentieth-century atheist philosopher Bertrand Russell was once asked what he would say if, upon death, he found himself face-to-face with God. Russell's answer was "Not enough evidence, God! Not enough evidence."

For many of us God can sometimes feel very present. Perhaps this happens from time to time in the context of a worship service where God's presence seems palpable. But it is not uncommon for us to go through periods when God feels entirely distant. It feels as if our prayers are hitting the ceiling, and no matter what we do, God is just not there.

For others God has never felt present. It seems if he exists, he's hiding. God could so easily reveal himself and even show off his power, but he doesn't. This experience of the absence or so-called hiddenness of God has led many to believe that God is not there at all. So the big question is if God is there, shouldn't he be more obvious?

A Hidden God

It's natural to think that if God is as good and as loving as the Bible pictures him to be, then he *should* show up in our lives in obvious ways. I, as an imperfect loving father, try to be there for my kids. That's meeting only minimal expectations of being a good parent. I show up for my kids. I would be failing as a parent if my kids had to wonder about my love and commitment to them. I try to remind them regularly that I love them and that I'm there for them when they need me. And I try to do things for them to show my love. But God often seems to not show up. God can seem very absent. This fact seems out of step with a loving God, especially when someone is deeply struggling and a simple reassurance that he's there is all they need. I fall short as a parent given my human limitations, but God has no such limitations. Since he's not as obvious as a loving God should be, it is argued that it's more reasonable to believe God does not exist.

Christians often immediately react to this by saying that for them God is extremely obvious. But the problem doesn't go away. All we have to do is consider the fact that many people question whether God exists. At least some of these, I take it, are genuinely questioning God's existence. So even if he seems extremely obvious for some, he's not obvious to all. Furthermore, God might be evident in some ways, but surely he could be *more* obvious than he is. He could supernaturally cause flashes of light in the sky spelling "Hey you! I am real. Love God" every time someone wonders whether he is there. God could do this. It's clear God could be more obvious than he is.

We have biblical examples of God being extremely obvious at times, but it's often very selective. God shows up to Moses in a burning bush despite the fact the bush is not being consumed (Exodus 3). It was obvious to Moses that God was there. In another instance Jesus blinds the eyes of Saul of Tarsus and speaks verbally saying, "I am Jesus," (Acts 9:5). Why couldn't the all-powerful God of the universe give all of us these sorts of experiences? Wouldn't this make a difference to a person like Bertrand Russell in his coming to believe? At least Russell couldn't say, "Not enough evidence."

How Obvious Must God Be?

If one thinks God should be obvious, how obvious must he be? It might be tempting to think that God must be *maximally* obvious. That is, God must fully manifest himself to all people at all moments. God in his great power could reveal himself this way and, so the thought is, if this would make a difference in the lives of people, he therefore should.

However, what if God has good reasons to veil himself? What if his full presence was actually lethal? When God first revealed himself to Moses, he did it through the medium of a burning bush. Later in Exodus, God would only let Moses see him from the backside after he had passed by. The reason is that if God revealed his full glory, then, as the Bible says, no human could live (Exodus 33:20). This is presumably because of human sin. God's full presence is lethal to sinful humanity. If this is true, then he *shouldn't* be maximally obvious if he loves us. If he did, it would kill us.

This shows that it is not easy to say just how obvious God must be. We may think that God should be obvious only to find out that it would be a very bad thing if he was. In theory we may want him to be that obvious, but perhaps there's a *really* good reason why he is not. If so, then the fact that God is not as obvious as we wish is not really a problem for belief.

Sometimes the thought is that God must be sufficiently obvious to preclude someone well-intentioned in seeking after God to disbelieve. But it is not entirely clear what it means to be well-intentioned in seeking after God. Bertrand Russell would perhaps fancy himself as being well-intentioned in this way. But Russell often seemed completely set against believing in God. TV host and comedian Bill Maher was once asked in an interview with Larry King whether he would believe if God spoke to him. His response, "No, if I thought the Lord was speaking to me, I'd check myself into Bellevue [psychiatric hospital], and I think you should too."[1] Maher's point was, in effect, this evidence would do nothing to convince him of the existence of God. He would conclude not that God exists but that he is having a psychotic episode. If an actual experience of God's voice would not convince Maher, then it's difficult to know what would.

This seems to be a clear instance of the vice of skepticism, discussed in chapter six, where there's a refusal to believe no matter the evidence. Skeptics are not looking for evidence, since their minds are completely made up that God does not exist and all religions are false. But even Bill Maher may say he'd believe if there was evidence. It's just not clear what sort of evidence, if any, he's genuinely open to.

But surely, we might think, some *would* believe if God was more obvious. That is, aren't there well-intentioned people who are genuinely open to the evidence? Here again, it's not entirely clear. The Bible suggests that the answer is no. Paul says, "There is no one who seeks God" (Romans 3:11). David, in Psalm 53:2-3 says, "God looks down from heaven on the human race to see if there is one who is wise, one who seeks God. All have turned away; all alike have become corrupt. There is no one who does good, not even one" (HCSB). The biblical idea seems to be that because of the corruption of our hearts, we are naturally set against believing in God. We are not, according to the Bible, innocent bystanders open to believing in God. We have a problem, and that is our sinful hearts. Thus it's at least plausible that we are naturally resistant to recognizing the reality of God.

God Is Sufficiently Obvious

God is, to a degree, obvious, or at least evident. Yes, he could be more obvious than he is, but God is also not completely veiled. Most people in the history of world have believed in some sort of God. This only makes sense if God is to some degree evident in the world. We looked in chapter seven at reasons to believe that God exists. This was only a sampling of the many aspects of creation that people take to be evidence of God. Romans 1:20 says that God can be "clearly seen" to the degree that "people are without excuse." The evidence is there, sufficient for belief but not to such a degree that it is coercive. If we are inclined to refuse to recognize the reality of God, then we will resist believing. To reference C. Stephen Evans again, the evidence for God is *widely available* but, at the same time, *easily resistible*.[2] So despite our natural resistance, the evidence of God is widely available.

Now, it's true, God could compel every human being to intellectually believe that he exists. But this should terrify us! Thankfully God, it seems, is not interested in compelling belief as a matter of coercion. Norwood Russell Hanson imagines this case:

Suppose…that next Tuesday morning, just after breakfast, all of us in this one world are knocked to our knees by a percussive and ear-shattering thunderclap. Snow swirls; leaves drop from the trees; the earth heaves and buckles; buildings topple and towers tumble; the sky is ablaze with an eerie, silvery light. Just then, as all the people of the world look up, the heavens open—the clouds pull apart—revealing an unbelievably immense and radiant-like Zeus figure, towering above us like a hundred Everests. He frowns darkly as lightning plays across the features of his Michelangeloid face. He then points down—*at* me!—and explains, for every man and child to hear: "I have had quite enough of your too-clear logic-chopping and word-watching in matters of theology. Be assured, N. R. Hanson, that I most certainly do exist." . . . If such a remarkable event were to occur, *I* for one should certainly be convinced that God does exist.[3]

Hanson is right that God could bring us all to our knees convinced that God exists. But would we really want this? Why think God is interested in this sort of a forced response? We should, in a way, be thankful that God is not interested in cowing us into belief. This is, to say the least, not a favorable situation.

Now we need to clarify what God is after in all of this. This might sound surprising but it's a mistake to think God's primary aim is to get someone to *believe* that he exists. God doesn't want mere intellectual belief. He wants believers who will follow him in faith. I'd even suggest that God would prefer people to not believe than for people to intellectually believe without faith. It seems God isn't particularly interested in having people who believe but then disregard and disobey the ways of God.

If this is what he was after, then God could easily achieve the goal of more belief. God could speak to people through burning bushes all over the world and blinding people with light as he audibly speaks to them. Or God could show up in other unmistakable and terrifying ways. There would probably be many more intellectual believers. The problem is this assumes God just wants intellectual believers.

Take, for example, the nation of Israel in the Old Testament. Israel's problem wasn't so much an intellectual problem of belief. It wasn't like the people kept struggling with doubts about the existence of Yahweh. It was a problem of behavior. They worshiped and followed other gods and neglected the one true God. Their problem was disobedience, especially relating to idolatry. It's easy to read these passages and wonder why they couldn't get their act together, especially given all they had seen. But it's because of a problem of the heart and not the intellect, not an issue of their knowledge but their obedience.

And again, as we discussed earlier, James tells us even the demons believe in God's existence and they shudder (James 2:19). James is saying that even the demons believe intellectually that there's a God, but they don't follow the way of God in faith.

Many people intellectually believe there's a God, but they also have not surrendered their lives to God. Their belief in God seems to make no difference to how they live. Many believers are, as it is sometimes said, functional atheists. Why would God want more functional atheists?

So while it may be the case that Bertrand Russell would perhaps intellectually believe if God was more obvious, there's no guarantee he would give his life in faith. God could be more obvious in showing his reality and power and many more people would believe, but it seems possible this would not fulfill the aim of God to have a people of faith.

The claim here is that God is sufficiently obvious in a way calibrated to his plan and his purposes for a people who follow him in faith. Could God compel more people to believe intellectually? Yes, more spectacular displays would turn this trick. But if this is not what he's after, then God would have good reasons to be somewhat veiled.

Many Believers but Few Followers

This seems to be what played out in the life of Christ. Jesus did many miraculous and spectacular things during his ministry. Did it make people believers? Yes, at least in a sense. People came from all over to see Jesus do his miraculous works. They intellectually believed he was something special. But it often didn't make people followers, or, in the language of the Gospels, it didn't make them disciples. They often didn't follow him by placing their trust in him. They just followed him around, eager for a more spectacular show. Once Jesus started talking about what it meant to follow him in discipleship, people often looked for the nearest exit.

In John 6 Jesus has a huge crowd of people who have gathered. But it appears they are there primarily to see a show. John 6:2 says, "A great crowd of people followed him because they saw the signs he had performed by healing the sick." A bit later in the passage we find out there were no less than five thousand men in this group. Presumably, this means there were upward of ten thousand people if we add in the women and the children who would have also been there. Then the need becomes obvious that the people do not have any food except one boy who has five loaves of bread and two fish. Jesus has the entire assembly sit down and begins to miraculously multiply the bread and the fish such that everyone has their fill, and there were twelve baskets of leftovers. The people are astonished, and they come to have beliefs about Jesus. They say, "Surely this is the Prophet who is to come into the world" (John 6:14).

Now, who wouldn't love getting free food and a show? They believe that he is the prophet. But the people want more of the show. A bit later on Jesus says some difficult things about who he is and what it means to follow him, and the people grumble. The people begin to desert him (John 6:66). No more fishes and loaves. Apparently, the show is over.

These people have all sorts of evidence to place their faith in Jesus. Many of them intellectually believe that he is a prophet, but they stop short of faith. Having the evidence of spectacular displays didn't make much difference. The people just wanted more spectacular displays.

Again, this isn't to say our intellectual beliefs are unimportant. We have to believe certain things to properly place our faith in Jesus. We cannot properly place our faith in Jesus if we believe he is just another finite and flawed moral teacher. The point is that God is after faith in light of proper beliefs about Jesus, not just the proper beliefs.

Faith and the Spectacular

As we think about it, the spectacular isn't very effective at bringing about genuine faith. When we experience the spectacular, it can be almost addictive and distracting. If we are not careful, it seems to have a tendency to draw us away from God. We start wanting more of that experience and lose sight of wanting more of God and all that this entails. Clearly, in the example of Jesus' miracles, we see people who are there for the show, and the miracles do not produce repentance and faith. The spectacular creates spectators, but it doesn't produce faith.

So why did Moses get a verbal speech from God through a burning bush and why did Saul of Tarsus (later the apostle Paul) get a blinding appearance of Jesus on the road to Damascus? The answer seems to be because of where their hearts were. That is, they were ready to have these experiences, and it wasn't coercive. Paul, in particular, came to see the error of his ways and had a humble heart in light of it.

Faith Comes from the Conviction of the Heart

The reality is that not many people believed in Jesus and became true followers during his lifetime. By the time of Jesus' ascension, he had only a fledgling following. But there is a certain point at which mass numbers of people come to place their faith in Jesus. It wasn't in the midst of miracles but in the midst of preaching the gospel. Throughout the book of Acts many thousands of people become true followers of Jesus as the disciples preach repentance. The disciples perform miracles in the book of Acts, but again the results of faith rarely come from this. The result of faith comes from hearing the gospel.

This is an important point. Miracles play a role in Jesus' ministry and the building of the church, but it is almost always a minor role. When they play a role, it is in support of the proclamation of the gospel. It is in the proclamation of the gospel that God works in the hearts of people, and they come to a place of conviction and repentance. On the day of Pentecost, the disciples are filled with the Holy Spirit and miraculously speak languages of the people who are gathered. But it's when Peter preaches the gospel that "they were cut to the heart" (Acts 2:37) and three thousand people come to faith!

Paul affirms the importance of God-sent preaching:

> How, then, can they call on the one they have not believed in? And how can they believe in the one of whom they have not heard? And how can they hear without someone preaching to them? And how can anyone preach unless they are sent? . . . But not all the Israelites accepted the good news. . . . Consequently, faith comes from hearing the message, and the message is heard through the word about Christ. (Romans 10:14-17)

Notice that faith does not necessarily come from experiencing fantastic miracles. If this is right, then faith comes from hearing, far more than it comes from seeing fantastical displays. And if God aims for people to be brought to faith rather than mere intellectual belief, then it seems plausible God is as obvious as he can be to accomplish his aim. If he was more obvious, it may produce more intellectual belief but it may produce fewer people of genuine faith.

Conclusion

Christianity as the Way

When you fall deeply in love . . . bemused friends may think,
"She's leading him around by the nose," but from the inside it feels
like heaven. For a Christian, it's the same with Jesus. The love of
Christ constrains. Once you realize how Jesus changed for you
and gave himself for you, you aren't afraid of giving up your
freedom and therefore finding your freedom in him.

TIMOTHY KELLER

Men despise religion; they hate it, and fear it is true.
To remedy this, we must begin by showing that religion is not
contrary to reason; that it is worthy of reverence and respect;
then we must make it attractive, to make good men wish it were
true; and then prove that it is true. Worthy of reverence because
it really understands human nature. Attractive because
it promises the true good.

BLAISE PASCAL

In the movie *Braveheart*, Mel Gibson plays William Wallace,
the thirteenth-century Scot who led the Scottish uprising
against British rule for the independence of Scotland. In one
scene of the movie Wallace gives a speech to motivate a ragtag

assembly of Scottish soldiers who showed up to the battlefield but were not willing to fight the superior English army. Wallace says, "I am William Wallace, and I see a whole army of my countrymen, here, in defiance of tyranny. You've come to fight as free men, and free men you are. What will you do without freedom? Will you fight?"

One of the reluctant soldiers says, "Fight? Against that [indicating the British army]? No! We will run! And we will live." Wallace responds,

Aye. Fight and you may die. Run, and you'll live . . . at least a while. And dying in your beds, many years from now, would you be willing to trade all the days, from this day to that, for one chance—[getting louder] just one chance—to come back here and tell our enemies that they may take our lives but they'll never take . . . [screaming] our freedom![1]

In the climax of the movie Wallace has been captured by the English and at the height of his torture is offered a chance for a merciful death. Just when his torturers and the gathered crowd think he is about to plead for mercy, Wallace defiantly screams once again "freedom," and this is the rallying cry of Scotland as it attempts to throw off the bondage of England.

Even if we have no idea about the history of Scotland, it seems impossible to not be inspired by these scenes. We love this kind of moment because we love freedom. We love stories about the struggle for freedom. Many high points of human history involved an individual or a group fighting for and gaining freedom from some sort of tyrannical rule or oppression. We have the Israelites gaining their freedom from slavery in Egypt in the exodus. We have the Emancipation Proclamation that freed thousands of slaves from the bondage of the brutal slavery of the United States. And we have the Allied victory over Nazi Germany and the freeing of the victims of the concentration camps, among many other examples.

By contrast, many people see Christianity as holding a kind of bondage over people. It is seen by some as both tyrannical and authoritarian. The Christian Bible indeed contains many rules. It prescribes a lifestyle we should live by. It gives us rules about sexuality, marriage, speech, work, worship, church, how to treat people, what to do with money, and so on. Many of the rules are seriously out of fashion with today's conventions and seem to only make sense to a bygone era. It's thought that many of its rules are so restrictive that even if Jesus rose from the dead, embracing Christianity would be a significant limit to our freedom.

I suggest this way of seeing Christianity is fundamentally wrong. Rather Christianity, if true, is the source of true freedom. As we've leaned in with our questions and doubts, my hope is that we find its truth. But it's not true in some theoretical sense. It prescribes a way of life that has our good in mind.

Rules That Bring Freedom

The perspective of the modern world is to throw off all constraints; any kind of limit to our freedom is bad by virtue of its constraints. Many today want freedom above all else, but is freedom always good? Should we want absolute freedom? My claim is that freedom from all constraints harms us. Absolute freedom, ironically, brings bondage.

At the basis of the Christian view are claims of universal truths of reality. Christianity purports to truly explain the world and how we should live in it. If it is true, then this is a game-changer. If, as Pascal says in the above epigraph, it "really understands human nature," then its attractive promise is our true good. My claim is that the way of freedom and flourishing is by conforming our lives to it. Jesus says, "You will know the truth, and the truth will set you free" (John 8:32). Jesus explicitly connects freedom with truth. The truth about reality sets us free!

Now you maybe didn't realize you needed to be set free. Jesus' Jewish audience responds by wondering who they were slaves to that necessitates being set free. Jesus responds, "Truly I tell you, everyone who sins is a slave to sin. . . . So if the Son sets you free, you will be free indeed" (John 8:34-36). The problem we have is a problem of corruption and fallenness.

The worldly perspective is that freedom is the freedom *to* sin. But the way of sin is the way of destruction. It's easy to sin. It takes very little effort. In Matthew 7:13-14, Jesus compares two different gates. One is wide and easy. But this gate leads to destruction. Freedom from all constraints is the broad and easy path, but it leads to harm and destruction. The other is narrow and difficult, but it leads to life.

Think about it. We need rules and constraints or we will not survive. Imagine if there were no rules when it came to eating. Our bodies are designed to eat in an overall healthy way or we will have problems. These are the facts we must abide by. Sure, there are those lucky few who can eat junk food whenever they want without gaining weight, but most of us can't do that, especially as we get older. And those who don't seem to gain weight aren't always particularly healthy when they eat in an excessively permissive way. And there are limits to what they can consume. They of course cannot ingest poison or large amounts of plastic. There are rules to eating that we must follow, and throwing off those rules in the name of absolute freedom will end in our destruction.

What if we do not like the restriction of healthy eating? The problem with this is that we become unhealthy. Once we have these health problems it becomes a kind of prison and bondage. And in the most extreme case, living outside the rules of healthy eating leads to our death. Throwing off the bounds of healthy eating may be a certain kind of freedom, but it's a freedom that only leads to harm and deep restriction.

The desire for freedom is legitimate when we desire freedom from things that harm us. We shouldn't only want freedom from any and all constraints, since some constraints are good for us. We should want freedom from things that harm well-being. We should want freedom from living under an oppressive tyrant's rule. This is not simply for freedom's sake but because it runs contrary to our design. It is counter to reality. Living under an oppressive tyrant is harmful and limits well-being. We celebrate and are inspired by William Wallace not simply because of freedom, but because he gave his life for freedom from living contrary to God's design for people.

Or, for another example, one rightfully desires freedom from slavery. For example, chattel slavery, where a human being is considered legal property, does not lead to well-being. Again, it's contrary to our design. We should oppose this constraint but not just because it is a constraint. We should oppose laws like this because they lead to deep harm for the enslaved (and arguably for the slaveholder as well). It is a system that is corrupting to all involved. We are not meant to own other human beings. Living under the rules of slavery in which human beings are reduced to the value of farm equipment is something we rightfully seek freedom from and celebrate liberty when it is found.

More generally, should we want absolute freedom when it comes to politics? Total anarchy—what is known in political philosophy as the "state of nature"—is not typically thought to be a good idea because it will likely lead to chaos and abuse. To avoid the state of nature we must surrender absolute freedom for the good of all. If you asked most people whether a person should be able to destroy someone else's property or physically harm someone just because they want to, the answer would be an emphatic no! People should be constrained against doing that. It seems we need some rule of law.

What we need are rules that are in accord with reality. Again, the truth sets us free. Ultimately, we need rules that lead to our well-being, and we want liberty from anything that leads to harm. Is there any doubt that staying away from illicit and highly addictive drugs is a good rule for life? Or not playing Russian roulette or driving 200 mph through a busy neighborhood or skydiving without a parachute? We run into the facts of reality rather quickly when we pursue absolute freedom from all constraints.

What is genuine freedom then? Dallas Willard makes a distinction between mere "freedom from" and freedom that's appropriate to the world we inhabit.[2] Freedom from is just freedom from constraints and, as we've seen, this can often be harmful to us. In fact, freedom from can result in our bondage. But genuine freedom comes not from throwing off constraints but from being conformed to reality as it is.

True freedom is best seen in examples of excellence. Take, for example, the professional athlete, expert musician, or accomplished scholar. We look up to these people and may even be a bit jealous of their lives. They are able to do things the rest of cannot. But how did they get to these places? By massively restricting their lives! The true experts have spent most of their lives attempting to conform themselves to the reality of their sport or discipline. The athlete must learn to shoot the ball or swing the bat according to the dictates of reality. Musicians can't just do whatever they want in playing their instrument. Expertise requires conforming, but conforming to reality. It's the truth that sets us free. Each of these gets to experience a level of freedom in their respective areas few of us get to experience because they have achieved excellence. Willard says:

> So, if we want to see freedom, we don't look at a kid jumping around with nothing to do. We see freedom when we see an accomplished artist sit down at a piano and play something so beautiful that we can hardly stay in our seat. That's freedom. When Pavarotti steps up and does what he does, the incredible magic—that's freedom.[3]

The task is to find out what reality is like.

Being an Apprentice of Jesus

Before Jesus says his famous line about knowing the truth and being set free as a result, he says, "If you hold to my teaching, you are really my disciples" (John 8:31); and it's with this that "You will know the truth, and the truth will set you free" (John 8:32). The claim here is that being a disciple or an apprentice of Jesus is the way to know the truth that sets us free. As Jesus puts it, "I am the way and the truth and the life" (John 14:6). This draws together why we should ask questions and lean into our doubts. By wandering toward God we find the way, the truth, and the life. As we place faith in Jesus, we are free from the bondage of sin and made right with God. By following Jesus and living by these truths, this leads to our well-being and flourishing. It leads to genuine freedom.

An Invitation to the Christian Journey

Christianity is radical among religious alternatives. It invites us to faith based on objective fact! It calls us to believe because it is true. This is quite extraordinary. It does not call for a blind intellectual leap in the darkness, and it also doesn't hold out salvation for a select enlightened few. All are welcome to consider the case for the Christian gospel.

We are going to have questions, some of which we don't know the answer to. We are going to need to ask these questions, and it's going to take courage to do so. This may get messy and that's okay. We may even doubt some of our Christian beliefs along the way. That's okay too.

When we have doubts, we shouldn't run from this. We don't need to have complete certainty, and we shouldn't aim at getting it. Instead, we should lean into our doubts and investigate those questions aiming at confidence. We can have confidence even if we have some unanswered questions. We can have confidence even if a few doubts remain. The goal is to find truth, and the truth will set us free.

On my journey, I have found answers, and my restless heart has found peace. I have taken the confident leap in venturing trust in Christ. I definitely don't have it all figured out, but I also don't doubt my faith as I did. I have found confidence in Christianity.

The Christian life is a journey, not simply a destination. We have a destination we are headed to, namely, the heavenly presence of God. For any journey worth going on, there's a significant cost involved. Worthy journeys also require considerable effort. It might even be painful at times. It's no fun to doubt. A lot is riding on these beliefs. But with the truth comes genuine freedom.

Christianity can handle the biggest questions and the hardest doubts. So journey on, and may your restless heart find its peace in the truth and reality of God.

Notes

1. Wandering but Not Lost

[1]J. R. R. Tolkien, *The Fellowship of the Ring* (Boston: Houghton Mifflin Co., 1954).

[2]Os Guinness, *God in the Dark: The Assurance of Faith Beyond a Shadow of Doubt* (Wheaton, IL: Crossway, 1996), 29.

[3]Guinness, *God in the Dark*, 26.

2. Doubt Defined

[1]See Gary Habermas's excellent book *Dealing with Doubt* (Chicago: Moody Publishing, 1990). Here he delineates a variety of forms of doubt.

[2]C. S. Lewis, *Surprised by Joy* (San Diego: Harvest, 1984), 228-29.

[3]Alister McGrath, *Doubting: Growing Through the Uncertainties of Faith* (Downers Grove, IL: InterVarsity Press, 2006), 18.

[4]Douglas J. Moo, *James*, Tyndale New Testament Commentaries, vol. 16 (Downers Grove, IL: InterVarsity Press, 2015), 87.

[5]Alvin Plantinga, *Warranted Christian Belief* (New York: Oxford University Press: 2000), 149.

[6]Frederick Buechner, *Wishful Thinking: A Seeker's ABC* (New York: HarperCollins, 1993), 23.

[7]Timothy Keller, *The Reason for God: Belief in an Age of Skepticism* (New York: Penguin, 2008), xvii.

[8]See, for example, Augustine's *Confessions*.

3. Certainty Is a House of Cards

[1]John Adams, letter to Abigail Adams, July 3, 1776, *NCpedia*, accessed February 16, 2020, www.ncpedia.org/media/letter-john-adams-abigail.

[2]René Descartes, *The Philosophical Writings of Descartes*, trans. John Cottingham, Robert Stoothoff, and Dugald Murdoch (New York: Cambridge, 1984), 2:12.

[3]Descartes, *Philosophical Writings of Descartes*, 15.

[4]Of course, if it's even just possible to have a dream that is as vivid as waking life, then the dream argument demolishes most of what we take ourselves to believe.

[5]Sheldon Vanauken, *A Severe Mercy: A Story of Faith, Tragedy and Triumph* (New York: HarperCollins, 1980), 98.

[6]Vanauken, *Severe Mercy,* 98.

4. The Virtue of Faith

[1]Mark Twain, *Following the Equator* (New York: Dover, 1989), 132.

[2]Richard Dawkins, speech, Edinburgh International Science Festival, April 15, 1992, quoted in Alister McGrath, *Christianity: An Introduction,* 2nd ed. (Malden, MA: Blackwell, 2006), 102.

[3]Sam Harris, *Letter to a Christian Nation* (New York: Vintage, 2008), 67.

[4]Peter Boghossian, *A Manual for Creating Atheists* (Durham, NC: Pitchstone, 2013), 23-24.

[5]J. P. Moreland, *Love Your God with All Your Mind: The Role of Reason in the Life of the Soul* (Colorado Springs, CO: NavPress, 2012), 70.

[6]Aristotle, *Nicomachean Ethics,* trans. Hippocrates G. Apostle (Des Moines, IA: Peripatetic Press, 1984), 142.

5. Doubt Your Doubts

[1]A portion of this section and the two that follow appeared in my article "Doubt as Virtue: How to Doubt and Have Faith Without Exploding," *Christian Research Journal* 39, no. 4 (2016), www.equip.org/article/doubt-virtue-doubt-faith -without-exploding.

[2]See Mary Jo Sharp, "Is the Story of Jesus Borrowed from Pagan Myths?" in *In Defense of the Bible: A Comprehensive Apologetic for the Authority of Scripture,* ed. Steven B. Cowan and Terry L. Wilder (Nashville, TN: B&H Academic, 2013).

[3]C. S. Lewis, *Christian Reflections* (Grand Rapids, MI: Eerdmans, 1995), 155.

[4]Blaise Pascal, *Pascal's Pensées* (New York: Dutton & Co., 1958), 52.

[5]Pascal, *Pensées,* 66.

[6]Pascal, *Pensées,* 66.

[7]Pascal, *Pensées,* 66.

[8]Peter Kreeft, *Christianity for Modern Pagans: Pascal's Pensées Edited, Outlined, and Explained* (San Francisco: Ignatius Press, 1993), 296.

6. Asking Big Questions

[1]Plato, *Plato: Five Dialogues,* trans. G. M. A. Grube (Indianapolis: Hackett, 2002), 41.

[2]G. K. Chesterton, *Illustrated London News,* October 10, 1908.

[3]C. S. Lewis, "On Reading Old Books," in Athanasius, *On the Incarnation* (New York: St Vladimir's Seminary Press, 1996), 4-5.

7. The Reason for God

[1]See Jerry Walls and Trent Dougherty, *Two Dozen (or so) Arguments for God: The Plantinga Project* (New York: Oxford University Press, 2018), for a book that explores the arguments Plantinga originally pointed at. This volume also contains Plantinga's original that was previously unpublished.

[2]C. Stephen Evans, *Natural Signs and the Knowledge of God: A New Look at Theistic Arguments* (New York: Oxford University Press, 2012), 12-17.

[3]For more see Geraint F. Lewis and Luke A. Barnes, *A Fortunate Universe: Life in a Finely Tuned Cosmos* (Cambridge, UK: Cambridge University Press, 2016); and Stephen C. Meyer, *Return of the God Hypothesis: Three Scientific Discoveries that Reveal the Mind Behind the Universe* (New York: HarperOne, 2021).

[4]For more see Hugh Ross, *Improbable Planet: How Earth Became Humanity's Home* (Grand Rapids, MI: Baker Books, 2016).

[5]Paul Davies, "Yes, the Universe Looks Like a Fix, but That Doesn't Mean God Fixed It," *Guardian*, June 25, 2007, www.theguardian.com/commentisfree/2007/jun/26/spaceexploration.comment.

[6]Albert Einstein, "Physics and Reality," *Daedalus* 132, no. 4 (2003): 23-24.

[7]Thomas Jefferson, et al, July 4, 1776, Copy of Declaration of Independence, www.loc.gov/item/mtjbib000159/.

[8]United Nations, "Article 1," Universal Declaration of Human Rights, December 10, 1948, www.un.org/en/about-us/universal-declaration-of-human-rights.

8. Something Extraordinary Happened

[1]Tacitus, *The Annals*, trans. C. H. Moore and J. Jackson (Cambridge, MA: Harvard University Press, 1962), 283.

[2]John Dominic Crossan, *Excavating Jesus: Beneath the Stones, Behind the Texts* (New York: HarperCollins, 2001), 254.

[3]Gerd Lüdemann, *The Resurrection of Jesus: History, Experience, Theology*, trans. John Bowden (Minneapolis, MN: Fortress, 1994), 38.

[4]Gary Habermas, "The Case for the Resurrection," in *To Everyone an Answer: A Case for the Christian Worldview*, ed. Francis J. Beckwith, William Lane Craig, and J. P. Moreland (Downers Grove, IL: InterVarsity Press, 2004), 184.

[5]For a sketch of a variety of Jewish messianic movements during the first and second centuries, see N. T. Wright, *The New Testament and the People of God* (Minneapolis, MN: Fortress, 1992), 175-81.

[6]N. T. Wright, "Jesus' Resurrection and Christian Origins," *Gregorianum* 83, no. 4, (2002): 623.

[7]For more see Michael R. Licona, *The Resurrection of Jesus: A New Historiographical Approach* (Downers Grove, IL: InterVarsity Press, 2010).

9. Our Deepest Longings

[1]Blaise Pascal, *Pascal's Pensées* (New York: Dutton & Co., 1958), 113.

[2]Peter Kreeft and Ronald K. Tacelli, *Handbook of Christian Apologetics: Hundreds of Answers to Crucial Questions* (Downers Grove, IL: InterVarsity Press, 1994), 80.

[3]Augustine, *Confessions*, trans. Vernon J. Bourke (Washington, DC: Catholic University of America Press, 1953), 3.4.7.

[4]Augustine, *Confessions*, 3.4.7.

[5]Pascal, *Pensées*, 113.

[6]Pascal, *Pensées*, 113.

[7]C. S. Lewis, *Surprised by Joy* (San Diego: Harvest, 1984), 170, 174.

[8]Lewis, *Surprised by Joy*, 18.

[9]Robert Hoyler, "The Argument from Desire," *Faith and Philosophy* 5, no. 1 (1988): 61.

[10]C. S. Lewis, *Mere Christianity* (Westwood, NJ: Barbour and Company, 1952), 115.

[11]Lewis, *Mere Christianity*, 115.

[12]Kreeft and Tacelli, *Handbook of Christian Apologetics*, 78.

[13]Peter Kreeft, *Heaven: The Heart's Deepest Longing* (San Francisco: Ignatius, 1989), 201.

[14]See Travis Dickinson, *Logic and the Way of Jesus: Thinking Critically and Christianly* (Nashville, TN: B&H Academic, 2022), chap. 10.

[15]Erik Wielenberg, *God and the Reach of Reason* (New York: Cambridge, 2008), 117.

[16]Wielenberg, *God and the Reach of Reason*, 118.

[17]C. S. Lewis, "The Weight of Glory" in *The Weight of Glory and Other Addresses*, ed. W. Hooper (New York: Simon and Schuster, 1996), 25-26.

10. Is the God of the Bible Good and Loving?

[1]Richard Dawkins, *The God Delusion* (Boston: Houghton Mifflin, 2006), 31.

[2]Paul Copan, *Is God a Moral Monster? Making Sense of the Old Testament God* (Grand Rapids, MI: Baker, 2011), 170.

11. Why Is There So Much Pain and Suffering?

[1]See Alvin Plantinga, *God, Freedom, and Evil* (Grand Rapids, MI: Eerdmans, 1977).

[2]Peter Kreeft, *Making Sense Out of Suffering* (Cincinnati, OH: Servant Books, 1986), 133.

[3]Kreeft, *Making Sense*, 133.

12. Why Isn't God More Obvious?

[1]Bill Maher, interview by Larry King on *Larry King Live*, August 11, 2005, https://transcripts.cnn.com/show/lkl/date/2005-08-11/segment/01.

[2]C. Stephen Evans, *Natural Signs and the Knowledge of God: A New Look at Theistic Arguments* (New York: Oxford University Press, 2012), 12-17.

[3]Norwood Russell Hanson, *What I Do Not Believe and Other Essays* (New York: Humanities Press, 1971), 313, quoted in Michael J. Murray, "Coercion and the Hiddenness of God," *American Philosophical Quarterly* 30, no. 1 (1993): 27.

Conclusion

[1]*Braveheart*, directed by Mel Gibson (Los Angeles: Paramount, 1995).

[2]Dallas Willard, "Nietzsche Versus Jesus Christ" in *A Place for Truth*, ed. Dallas Willard (Downers Grove, IL: InterVarsity Press, 2010), 164-65.

[3]Williard, "Nietzsche Versus Jesus Christ," 165.